ASIA

PACIFIC OCEAN

INDIAN OCEAN

AUSTRALIA

MALAPACAO ISLAND IN THE
BACUIT ARCHIPELAGO,
THE PHILIPPINES

LONELY PLANET'S

BEST IN TRAVEL

2013

THE BEST TRENDS, DESTINATIONS, JOURNEYS & EXPERIENCES FOR THE UPCOMING YEAR

lonely planet

MELBOURNE ○ OAKLAND ○ LONDON

TOP TRAVEL LISTS 142

40 YEARS of TRAVEL!

2013 IS FULL OF AMAZING TRAVEL OPPORTUNITIES BUT IT WILL ALSO BE A YEAR IN WHICH LONELY PLANET CELEBRATES 40 YEARS OF TRAVEL. WE'VE ASKED CO-FOUNDER TONY WHEELER AND FIVE OTHER TRAVEL-GUIDE GURUS FOR THEIR TAKE ON WHAT THE LAST 40 YEARS HAVE MEANT.

TONY WHEELER
CO-FOUNDER, LONELY PLANET

Why do I travel? Because it's never boring. It can be uncomfortable at times – but never boring.

The 'I want to go there' list just keeps getting longer. The more places you go the bigger the world seems to get.

Travel doesn't really start with your first trip, because every kid discovers that travel with parents is never real travel.

It's only when you get out on your own that you really *travel* and those first solo teenage expeditions never leave you.

I lived in Pakistan with my parents when I was very small and there are so many clear memories – camels, beggars, magicians, jellyfish on the beach, fishing for crabs from a dhow on Karachi harbour, monsoon floods, vultures, an episode with a rabid dog – and all those memories must have been by the time I was five years old, because that's how old I was when I left.

My Dad – who was an RAF pilot – worked for BOAC (which became British Airways) so I was definitely going to be a pilot. I never did, but I can't

understand why I never got around to at least getting a pilot's licence.

Sir Joseph Banks was the rich, young and endlessly curious scientist who accompanied Captain Cook on his first great voyage. So many times that amazing trip was like a real-life *Close Encounter of the Third Kind.* If I had a time machine that's where it would take me, back on board HMS *Endeavour.*

Travel starts when you leave the airport, dump the pre-booked hotel and get off the tour bus, when there's nobody holding your hand any longer. Up to that point you've been a tourist.

> **I SOMETIMES THINK ANTARCTICA TOPS THE LOT. IT'S A CONTINENT OF ABSOLUTES, EVEN THE COLOURS ARE UTTERLY ABSOLUTE, EVERYTHING IS EITHER BLUE OR BLACK OR WHITE, NOTHING FALLS IN BETWEEN.**
>
> — TONY WHEELER —

Today's technology doesn't change travel into mere tourism. Recently I've crossed from one country (the Solomon Islands) to another (Papua New Guinea) in a small village boat. Did it matter that my GPS could show me where I was and how much more sea we had to cross?

You could earn a university degree from travel, I've learnt so much stuff about so many things.

If I hadn't got into travel publishing perhaps I'd have ended up a travel guide.

I'd be a lousy guide in some ways. I'd quickly lose all patience with people who want their hand held and their luggage lifted off the carousel, but I find when I'm with people I do a pretty good job (if I say so myself!) of explaining things in an interesting fashion.

For a long time now I've tried to spend at least one week each year exploring on foot and although I've not managed that every year, last year I spent nearly a month on multi-day walks in South Korea, Israel and Nepal. As well as the day walks.

I have to admit, I do love the view from airline windows.

I've often said my favourite place is the airport departure lounge, because it means you're about to go somewhere.

I have two homes and when I'm home in Melbourne (the bigger house) I never miss the home in London (the smaller one). Or vice versa. When I'm on the road I don't miss either.

When I do get home, to either home, about six weeks is the maximum I can take before my itchy feet want to head off somewhere else.

I sometimes think Antarctica tops the lot. It's a continent of absolutes, even the colours are utterly absolute, everything is either blue or black or white, nothing falls in between.

If there's a golden rule of travel, it's to leave your preconceptions at home, however far you've gone down the road you're still likely to meet somebody who has gone even further.

How you travel and who you travel with – these can change from trip to trip. There's no right way, no right combination. **When I started out** it was all about shoestring travel, making your money go as far as it could.

There are so many travel experiences that only money can buy. These days I don't worry about costs, but I haven't lost sight of the value of experiences that only travelling close to street level (on street costs) can bring you.

Travelling alone, you meet people you wouldn't meet if you were already with somebody else and you certainly never have any arguments about what you should be doing!

Travel with kids can be a strain, but it's amazing how they open doors for you. In lots of places an offspring or two can instantly convert you from just another tourist to a real human being.

For me travel has been a job as well as a pleasure for so long it's hard to separate the two reasons for my travelling. Even when I don't need to I can't help taking notes, 'somebody might like to know about that restaurant, that great shortcut, that interesting new museum, that great bar.'

I'm always looking forward to the next trip, there's always a wish list and sometimes it amazes me how long things have been on that 'must do' list. Why have I never travelled across Russia on the Trans-Siberian Express?

I never really thought of it as work, I reckon I'd have paid to have my job.

STEFAN LOOSE
FOUNDER, STEFAN LOOSE GUIDES

Our parents travelled only where the world spoke German but the post-war generation used their school English to discover the world. They'd had enough of German society's stuffy atmosphere in the 1960s and they just pulled out, always a little further, going overland to Italy, Ibiza, Morocco, and then India and Nepal – the world seemed limitless. Those who returned months or even years later told their friends about their adventures and gave tips for the trip. And some made notes and had them printed.

In the 1970s, more than a dozen 'one author-one book' publishers came into existence with titles like *The Cheapest Trip to India, Afghanistan and Nepal* or *Africa for Self-Driving*. The flippantly written texts were peppered with spelling mistakes and hand-drawn maps but they were also packed with insider tips and concrete information about cheap places to sleep. They were very practical and up-to-date.

In 1975 during a garden party in Berlin some travellers founded a club, the 'German Centre for Globetrotters'. In their magazine, *Trotter,* they published travel stories and an event calendar. Once a year, insiders and newcomers met, slept in tents, cooked together and exchanged experiences.

The oil crises of 1973 and 1979, regional wars in Afghanistan and new complicated visa rules made overland travelling more arduous. Student travel agencies

discovered the grey market for cheap airline tickets. Now, you could travel to distant places for a short time without giving up career and home. Guidebooks became increasingly professional and the authors of the alternative guides, now in regular jobs, had no time to update their books. It didn't take long till their guides disappeared from the shelves. Many pioneers of the 1960s and 1970s have retired but their passion for travelling remains. The *Trotter* still exists, publishing the exploits of globetrotters, mountaineers and motorcyclists. Others, like me, turned their hobby into a career.

The founder of Stefan Loose Verlag, Stefan is working with Help Tourism in Kolkata and is currently fundraising for a school in Eastern Arunachal.

MARK ELLINGHAM
FOUNDER, ROUGH GUIDES

I set up Rough Guides as a 22-year-old, fresh out of university. I wrote about Greece because I liked the place and had noticed there wasn't a decent guidebook to be found. Not one that reflected my interests, anyway. I wanted a survival guide, with decent tips on living cheap, but also a book that opened up contemporary life and culture and politics. Greece was only five years out of the Colonels' dictatorship yet the other guides seemed to cut off somewhere around the fall of Byzantium. And nobody seemed to think we travellers might want to experience local festivals, music clubs and the like. **I hadn't heard of Lonely Planet** at the time because I hadn't been to southeast Asia, where that original yellow bible was making waves. But I met Tony Wheeler the year we published *Greece*. He had just brought out an awesome tome on India. 'Are you going to keep covering Europe?' Tony asked. 'Our focus is Asia.' And for the best part of a decade we had an unspoken detente, until we each ran out of space on the map. LP moved into the Mediterranean. Rough Guides set off for China.

> **I LIKE TO THINK WE HELPED SHAPE AN ATTITUDE THAT TRAVEL COULD BE A GOOD THING. YOU COULD SPREAD YOUR MONEY AROUND LOCAL ENTERPRISES AND TREAT PEOPLE WITH RESPECT AND CURIOSITY...**
>
> — MARK ELLINGHAM —

In retrospect, we were all hugely lucky. Guidebooks had fallen into a generational black hole. The good early ones – the Baedekers – had disappeared after the war, tarnished by the Nazis. Their place had been taken by the banalities of Frommer's five-dollars-a-day and the mid-budget platitudes of Fodor's. It was a space for new punks on the block. And so was the world. **Was there ever a better decade for travel than the 1980s?** Cheap(er) flights brought places like Peru or Zimbabwe (fun, post-Independence) or Nepal within reach of us Europeans, while Eastern Europe and China were opening their gates. It was a thrill producing a guide to a country that had never previously been

covered and drawing up the first decent – well, half-decent – maps. Guidebooks had powerful knowledge. I like to think we helped shape an attitude: that travel could be a good thing. You could spread your money around small, local enterprises. Treat people with a respect and curiosity perhaps lacking in previous generations of Western travellers. Maybe even give something back by getting involved in local projects and charities.

The guidebook is supposed to be in crisis, crushed by the free knowledge of Wikipedia, Google, Twitter, Facebook, or the tiresome complaints of TripAdvisor. But I'm not so sure about crisis. I think it's more like a transition. Sure, we've all gone crazy for social media, for someone telling us they went to a bar – just now! – and how great it is. But we also want a take on, say, Tangier or Budapest or Amsterdam, from someone who has scratched below their surface. And, of course, social networks aren't very useful for places where nobody is tweeting. What's hot in Kigali, anyone? **My hope for travel is that it becomes slower and longer.** We don't need to burn up CO_2 ticking off a mass of destinations. Far better a month or a year's travel in one place, taking time to become a part of it, getting the language and the culture. That could be Greece or India, those first Rough/LP destinations. Though if I was setting off, right now, for an extended trip, I'd head for Africa, where things are changing fast and generally for the better.

To Addis, then ... and beyond.

HILARY BRADT
CO-FOUNDER, BRADT GUIDES

The focus of our 1970s travels in South America was backpacking in the original American sense of the word – hiking for several days in the wilderness, carrying all our needs on our back. It was the questions from other gringos about 'how' and 'where' that prompted us to write a little book about five routes (including the now-famous Inca Trail) in Peru and Bolivia. The opportunity came when we took a river barge for three days down a tributary of the Amazon. At the Bolivian jungle town of Trinidad we borrowed a typewriter and George (my ex-husband) typed it up and sent it to his mother to print in Boston. It retailed for $1.95. And that, we thought, was that.

The internet has made an incalculable difference in the way we travel. In the Olden Days, George and I would get off the bus and, while one guarded the luggage, the other looked for a hotel. The cheap ones were always near the bus station so it was never a problem. These days most travellers will have booked at least their first night's accommodation online.

The backpacker hostel that doesn't have a website is doomed to failure.

I sometimes miss our total ignorance of what to see! I was never as bad as a friend who drove through Italy in the 1960s. 'There's a town here called Firenze', she told her boyfriend, 'should we stop, do you think?' 'Never heard of it', he responded. And so they continued south.

George and I were almost as clueless about Ecuador and Peru, but we learned to look at postcards to find out which sights the towns prided themselves on. It worked pretty well. If we spotted other gringos – a startling occurrence which happened infrequently – we would make a beeline in order to learn of their recommendations of places to stay and things to do. We realised that the clever thing was to travel from south to north, so we could tap into the

> **IT WAS THE QUESTIONS FROM OTHER GRINGOS ABOUT 'HOW' AND 'WHERE' THAT PROMPTED US TO WRITE.**
>
> — HILARY BRADT —

experiences of the majority of travellers going the other way.

One very noticeable attribute of travel today is the rise in responsible travel. Backpackers in the 1960s and '70s were ever ready to sneak into game parks or museums – and out of hotels – without paying. They boasted about it; in those hippy days it was the badge of an experienced

traveller. It sounds po-faced but it was not something I was comfortable with, so the rise of Tourism Concern and the general concept of travelling responsibly has come as a relief. It is a much better world for our host nations these days; and that's certainly something to celebrate.

Hilary Bradt is the co-founder and director of Bradt Travel Guides. She wrote her first book in 1974 and continues to write and lecture widely on travel.

TREMAYNE CAREW POLE
FOUNDER, A HEDONIST'S GUIDE

I love cities. I love getting under their skin and finding experiences that you wouldn't normally find in a weekend away. And I hate looking like an outsider when I visit. People treat you differently. We've always wanted readers to explore local neighbourhoods. Others do the practical information or the history very well. We specialise in a city's decadent side – it's all about comfortable beds, great food, the best parties.

The idea for the Hedonist's Guides came after a frustrating weekend in Budapest. I went away with a group of friends and we couldn't find the right places to eat or drink and wasted a weekend. At that time there was nothing that focused purely on where to eat, stay and play. I quit my job and moved to Prague to research the first book.

I had no writing, travel or publishing experience so it was a huge learning curve.

I had to go through the whole process for myself. You can't tell others what to do and how to do it if you haven't done it yourself first. We started off with second tier destinations – we felt we couldn't compete on London, New York, Paris – and went for smaller ones like Marrakech, Madrid, Tallinn, Beirut. The selection process is fairly arbitrary and there is no set formula.

A guidebook is a companion, a faceless friend who takes your hand and leads you through a new city. Travellers want an experience from a guidebook, they want a story to tell not just a slideshow of historical monuments. Thirty years ago it was about the monuments, today it is about the experience and Tony Wheeler was the person who gave the idea of getting off the beaten track to a generation. He has opened up the world to so many people.

In recent years I have moved away from everyday tourism and started going to slightly edgier, back-of-beyond destinations and meeting politicians and business people. I enjoy trying to understand what makes a country and people tick.

I loved Freetown, Sierra Leone. I had no preconceptions but we ended up having the most monumental week seeing everything the country had to offer. I love that tingling feel of not knowing what to expect when you land somewhere.

Tremayne Carew Pole founded the A Hedonist's Guide to...series in 2004.

BILL DALTON
FOUNDER, MOON PUBLICATIONS

Ever since the doors of an old prop plane were flung open in downtown Jakarta 40 years ago, I've been intrigued by the complexity, the diversity and the mystique of Indonesia. As a wall of suffocating heat and dust mixed with the smells of diesel and clove cigarettes rushed into the cabin, my first thought was: 'I love this place!'

Walking onto the hot tarmac of the old Kebayoran Airport that day was to ultimately lead to my whole professional life writing about this maddening, fascinating country. It started with the publication of six mimeographed pages of gypsy traveller's notes and crude handmade maps, stapled together and sold in the flea markets of Australia, and it culminated two decades later in the 6th edition of the *Indonesia Handbook*, a 1000-page behemoth and the first comprehensive guidebook on Indonesia published in the post-war period.

There was a time when one lone, determined guidebook writer – red-faced and sweat-drenched at the end of each day – could actually cover this sprawling string of islands during one three-month trip, working without competition for royalties and retaining full copyright ownership. But by the early 1990s, with the country's infrastructure exploding, competing guidebooks arrived and it became impossible for just one writer to research all of Indonesia. Instead, teams of writers were assigned to regions. Travel guidebooks have since metamorphosed into smartphone apps, but I still believe that disciplined professionals give the best obtainable version of the truth.

I glean fresh information from other travellers met along the way or from historical novels, which give more of a feel for the subtleties of the culture and the character of the people. If writers

> ### THE EXTREMITIES OF INDONESIA'S ARCHIPELAGO STILL OFFER HIGH ADVENTURE STRAIGHT OUT OF A JOSEPH CONRAD NOVEL.
> — BILL DALTON —

lavish too much praise on a hotel, beach or locale, I hit the other direction to avoid places that have been sabotaged by their own success. It beats the hell out of throwing a dart at a map on a wall.

The extremities of Indonesia's archipelago still offer high adventure, right out of a Joseph Conrad novel. In the far-flung southeastern islands, crew members onboard your *perahu* wear bandanas and stick knives in their belts, and a bottle of rice wine and a fellow traveller's yarn will lead you through the night like the North Star.

Bill Dalton founded Moon Publications in a youth hostel in Queensland. He published the *Indonesia Handbook* in 1973 and now lives with his Indonesian wife on a farm in West Bali.

LONELY PLANET'S
TOP 10
COUN
TRIES

by Brett Atkinson

'Indian and Thai cuisine may be world-renowned, but Sri Lanka's time in the global gourmet spotlight can't be far away'

○ SRI LANKA

#1

OFF-ROAD | VALUE | CULTURE

SRI LANKA

- ○ **POPULATION** 20.6 million
- ○ **FOREIGN VISITORS PER YEAR** 900,000
- ○ **CAPITAL** Colombo
- ○ **LANGUAGES** Sinhala, Tamil, English (unofficial)
- ○ **MAJOR INDUSTRIES** Tourism, tea, textiles and apparel
- ○ **UNIT OF CURRENCY** Sri Lankan Rupee (LKR)
- ○ **COST INDEX** Rice and curry lunch packet LKR200 (US$1.65), bottle of Lion Lager LKR250 (US$2), guesthouse in Ella LKR4000 (US$33), entrance to the rock fortress of Sigiriya LKR3900 (US$30)

WHY GO IN 2013? SERENITY RETURNS TO SERENDIB

Dubbed Serendib – the origin of the word serendipity – by seafaring Arab traders centuries ago, Sri Lanka has been anything but serene in recent decades. Battered tragically by the 2004 Boxing Day tsunami and wracked by civil war from 1983 to 2009, many areas of South Asia's most compact country have remained off limits to even the most intrepid traveller. Now the bitter conflict is over, investment is fuelling the tourism industry, and visitor numbers are steadily increasing. Prices are affordable, and with low-cost flights from the convenient travel hub of Bangkok, Sri Lanka is emerging as one of the planet's best-value destinations.

North of Colombo on Sri Lanka's west coast, Kalpitiya and the Puttalam lagoon are ecotourism hotspots with birdwatching and kayaking, and near Dondra Head on the south coast, mighty blue whales are regular visitors from January to April. Land-based wildlife thrills include the leopards and elephants of Yala National Park, and the more rugged and remote Wilpattu National Park, open again after being closed for more than two decades by the Sri Lankan civil war.

The gloriously arcing beaches of the nation's east coast are now challenging traditional southern favourites. Arugam Bay's sandy crescent is one of Asia's best surf spots, and further north, Uppuveli and Nilaveli near Trincomalee stretch for several pristine kilometres. Fast-forward five years, and both beaches will definitely be accorded 'Where to go next' status in the glossy travel magazines. Why wait that long?

LIFE-CHANGING EXPERIENCES

Explore the glorious labyrinth of Galle's 17th-century Dutch fort. In past centuries, the Unesco-listed colonial town was a prosperous hub of global trade, and now boutique hotels and an emerging arts scene instil a cosmopolitan allure. Further north, discover Sri Lanka's imposing Ancient Cities, now emerging from a verdant landscape. All around the country, tuck into great-value local food including grilled seafood, spicy *kotthu* (roti chopped and mixed with vegetables) and multicourse mini banquets of different curries at family-run guesthouses. Indian and Thai cuisine may be world-renowned, but Sri Lanka's time in the global gourmet spotlight can't be far away.

FESTIVALS & EVENTS

✪ Celebrate the enduring impact of the printed word at January's annual Galle Literary Festival. Past bookish visitors to the heritage fort town's storied streets include Orhan Pamuk, Pico Iyer and Alexander McCall Smith.

✪ In July, the annual Kataragama festival draws thousands of Hindu devotees at the completion of their multiweek Pada Yatra walking pilgrimage through rugged eastern Sri Lanka.

✪ Held annually around July/August, Kandy's Esala Perahera honours the sacred tooth of the Buddha held in the city's Temple of the Scared Tooth Relic. The festival culminates on the tenth and final night when dancers, drummers and around 50 lavishly decorated elephants parade through Kandy's narrow, lakeside streets.

HOT TOPIC OF THE DAY

Overseas investment, especially from China, is transforming the skyline of Colombo. Planned to open in 2013, the Colombo Lotus Tower will soar 350m from the oceanfront near Beira Lake. Throughout 2013, construction will be continuing on the new Shangri La Colombo hotel overlooking nearby Galle Face Green. Don't worry, there are still plenty of laid-back guesthouses on Sri Lanka's southern and eastern beaches.

RANDOM FACTS

✪ Rapper and hip-hop artist MIA, aka Mathangi Arulpragasam, is of Sri Lankan Tamil descent, and spent part of her childhood in the northern city of Jaffna during the Sri Lankan civil war.

✪ At the Millennium Elephant Foundation near Kandy, elephant dung is used to make stationery, books and greeting cards. All the products are definitely odour-free.

✪ Sri Lanka is one of the world's top tea producers, and accommodation in the nation's cool-climate Hill Country includes former tea factories and gracious colonial plantation houses.

MOST BIZARRE SIGHT

Rising from a halo of forest, Sigiriya rock boldly punctuates the landscape of central Sri Lanka. The route ascending Sigiriya is studded with risqué centuries-old paintings and graffiti, and atop the rock, the remains of gardens and pools are a reminder of its past as a temple or palace.

BATH TIME FOR
THE ELEPHANTS AT
ANURADHAPURA

by Andrea Schulte-Peevers

NORTH
AMERICA

EUROPE
⊙ MONTENEGRO

ASIA

AUSTRALIA

'Nature has been as prolific and creative here as Picasso in his prime...'

#2

ACTIVITIES | ADVENTURE | OFF-ROAD

MONTENEGRO

- ⊙ **POPULATION** 657,000
- ⊙ **FOREIGN VISITORS PER YEAR** 1.2 million
- ⊙ **CAPITAL** Podgorica
- ⊙ **LANGUAGE** Montenegrin
- ⊙ **MAJOR INDUSTRIES** Tourism, agriculture
- ⊙ **UNIT OF CURRENCY** Euro (€)
- ⊙ **COST INDEX** Glass of beer €1.50 (US$2), budget hotel double €20-30 (US$20-40), two-course meal €8-20 (US$10-26), burek (meat- or spinach- filled pastry) €1 (US$1.30)

WHY GO IN 2013? TAMING A WILD BEAUTY

When it ccmes to tourism, Montenegro is a country on the fast track to superstardom. Nature has been as prolific and creative here as Picasso in his prime, producing such iconic draws as the bewitching Bay of Kotor and the buzzy beaches along its Riviera. But be sure to pack a pair of hiking boots along with your swimsuit, for Montenegro's beauty is no less intense in the wild and rugged interior. Fierce mountains loom over velvety valleys, glacial lakes, precipitous canyons and dreamy villages where life unfolds much the way it has throughout history. A new – and steadily growing – network of hiking and biking trails and improved infrastructure is making this glorious quilt of nature ever more accessible, while creating new employment for locals.

Back on the coast, the government's eagerness to roll out the red carpet to foreign investors has resulted in such high-profile developments as Porto Montenegro, a luxury yacht marina and waterfront community in Tivat, and the restored glamour resort of Sveti Stefan near Budva. Independent only since 2006, Montenegro is also keen on becoming a full-fledged member of the international community and has applied for membership in the European Union and NATO.

LIFE-CHANGING EXPERIENCES

Montenegro's five national parks spotlight its most breathtaking natural features. Explore the country's 'upper storey' in dramatic Durmitor National Park, where the soaring peaks harbour bears and wolves, and also offer ski slopes and Europe's deepest gorge, the Tara Canyon, a rafters' paradise. In nearby Biogradska Gora National Park, a ramble through primeval forest leads to an alpine lake shimmering in countless shades of blue. It's feathered critters galore in water lily-fringed Lake Skadar National Park, Europe's biggest bird reserve. Brave the white-knuckle drive up to Lovćen National Park and you'll be rewarded with vistas across the entire country. The newest national park, untamed and remote Prokletije, on the border with Albania, boasts some of the highest mountains in the Balkans.

FESTIVALS & EVENTS

✪ In early August, the streets of Kotor erupt in song, dance and merriment during the International Summer Carnival, which culminates in a grand parade and all-night street party.

✪ Adventure racers from around the world test their skills kayaking, rafting, biking and high-roping through remote backcountry during October's 48-hour Montenegro

LACE UP YOUR HIKING BOOTS
TO EXPLORE DURMITOR
NATIONAL PARK

HOT TOPIC OF THE DAY

The economy, social inequality and corruption. In 2012, thousands of Montenegrins took to the streets to protest against economic woes, including soaring energy prices, regional discrepancies and unemployment. The protestors perceived the government as corrupt and catering primarily for the interests of local tycoons and foreign investors. Strong interest in joining the EU and NATO, however, has propelled the government to adopt a number of anticorruption laws and initiatives.

RANDOM FACTS

✪ Lovćen National Park is home to Crna Gora or Black Mountain, which gave Montenegro its name.

✪ The water of the Tara River is clean enough to drink.

✪ Montenegro has more than 150 mountains higher than 2000m.

✪ Lake Skadar, which is below sea level, is a rare nesting site of the endangered Dalmatian pelican.

✪ Montenegro has no minimum legal drinking age.

Expedition Challenge, one of Europe's most gruelling endurance races.

✪ Budva goes dramatic in July and August during the Budva Theatre City festival, featuring plays, classical music, art exhibits and poetry readings.

RECENT FAD

After you've baked in the sun all day, drag your bronzed self to an 'after-beach party' and watch the sun dip into the Adriatic as you dance with hundreds of other hedonistic revellers. Throughout the summer, some 300 such parties take over the seaside resorts, sometimes helmed by such DJ royalty as David Guetta, Sam Divine and Jamie Lewis.

MOST BIZARRE SIGHT

Right in the heart of the mountain resort of Kolašin looms one of the finest vestiges of socialist architecture from the Yugoslav era: the Memorial Hall, a futuristic concrete pile of triangles, cubes and other geometric shapes. It was designed in 1976 by Slovenian architect Marko Mušič to commemorate the town's role as centre of partisan resistance during WWII. Although badly in need of a makeover, it's currently home to municipal offices and may be converted into a congress centre.

by Rob Whyte

NORTH AMERICA

EUROPE

ASIA

☼ **SOUTH KOREA**

AFRICA

SOUTH

AUSTRALIA

'You'll earn top bragging rights after cruising the world's most dangerous bike path'

#3

🏃 ACTIVITIES | 🔷 OFF-ROAD | ✨ EVENTS

SOUTH KOREA

- ☼ **POPULATION** 48.9 million
- ☼ **FOREIGN VISITORS PER YEAR** 9.8 million
- ☼ **CAPITAL** Seoul
- ☼ **LANGUAGE** Korean
- ☼ **MAJOR INDUSTRIES** Electronics, shipbuilding, auto manufacturing, steel
- ☼ **UNIT OF CURRENCY** Korean won
- ☼ **COST INDEX** Cafe latte 3500 won (US$2.65), green fees, 18 holes, public golf course 170,000 won (US$150), screen golf, 18 holes per person 15,000 won (US$13), budget motel room 40,000 won (US$35)

DRINKING FOUNTAIN AND LADLES AT
BONGEUNSA BUDDHIST TEMPLE,
GANGNAM-GU, SEOUL

WHY GO IN 2013? TO ENJOY THE GREAT OUTDOORS

Think South Korea is just another high-density As an country filled with towers, temples and traffic? Think again. Without fanfare, South Korea has quietly developed into an outdoor recreation destination. Though not quite undiscovered, few people outside the Hermit Kingdom know about it. That anonymity will likely fade away in 2013 as the country bursts onto the world stage with three international sporting events.

So why visit in 2013? Because golfing, hiking and fishing, the country's three hottest outdoor pastimes, are South Korea's untapped gems – until now. With more than 100 golf courses, some designed by noteworthy architects like Jack Nicklaus, finding a course to test your mettle won't be a challenge. If you can't get – or afford – a tee time, try screen golf. Use real clubs and balls to drive, pitch and putt and let the computer take care of the rest.

Of course, you'll want to experience Seoul, a high-energy mega-city where skyscrapers chisel the skyline, Buddhist compounds offer a place for reflection and traffic is a code word for organised chaos. And when the din of urban commotion starts to overwhelm you, as it most certainly will, follow the Korean lead: grab your gear and escape. Pristine hiking trails on South Korean islands provide four seasons of solitude and breathtaking scenery with just enough

THE HEART OF SEOUL BY NIGHT

commercial development to make your stay comfortable. How's the fly fishing? Cast for cherry trout, lenok and river tarpon in splendid isolation amid an immaculate natural environment that moves even the crustiest of souls to ponder the magnificence of the universe.

LIFE-CHANGING EXPERIENCE

You'll earn top bragging rights after cruising the world's most dangerous bike path. Running alongside the demilitarised zone (DMZ) separating North and South Korea – the world's most fortified border – the scenery shifts between picturesque and surreal as you pedal past well-preserved biodiversity, barbed wire and landmines. The 18km path starts in Paju and is open two Sundays per month. If biking seems too much like work, walking tours can take you for a guided excursion along one section of the DMZ's razor-wire fencing.

FESTIVALS & EVENTS

✪ In January and February, Pyeongchang hosts the Special Olympics Winter Games. There will be 3300 athletes competing in 32 events including skiing and snowboarding. It's South Korea's largest ever winter sporting event and a warm-up for the much bigger 2018 Pyeongchang Winter Olympics.
✪ Bowlers, brawlers and gamers converge on Incheon for the 4th Annual Asian Indoor and Martial Arts Games from 29 June to 6 July. It's an eclectic mix of competition with no shortage of physically demanding contests like muay thai fighting, kickboxing and sport dancing (all that smiling can't be easy). It's another warm-up event as Incheon gets ready to stage the 2014 Asian Games.

✪ Sculls and coxes will be floating on Tangeum Lake as Chungju hosts the World Rowing Championship. From 24 August to 1 September, 2300 athletes and coaches from 80 countries will compete in 27 events.

RECENT FAD

Low-cost air travel. Five budget airlines now offer cheap seats (eg US$165 for a return ticket to Hong Kong) to an ever-growing number of Asian destinations, with frequent service to China, Japan, Thailand, Taiwan and the Philippines. In 2011 the number of domestic and international passengers on budget flights topped a record 10 million.

WHAT'S HOT...

Studying abroad, *makgeolli* (fermented rice wine), ebooks

...WHAT'S NOT

Studying in Korea, wine, print books

HOT TOPIC OF THE DAY

North Korea is always topical. Dear Leader, Kim Jong-il, is long gone and the country is waiting to see if the new regime (including Kim Jong-un as the supposed leader) will continue the north's tradition of alternating between military provocation and conciliation.

MOST BIZARRE SIGHT

Love Land on Jeju Island is a park where statues of giant penises and nude women come together in an inspiring display of x-rated positions. It's all for educational purposes, mind you: Jeju Island is South Korea's honeymoon capital.

by Luke Waterson

'....Ecuador's real lure: you can be in the high Andes one minute, and either in the Amazon jungle or on the beach a few hours later'

○ ECUADOR
SOUTH
AMERICA

#4

ACTIVITIES | OFF-ROAD | FOOD

ECUADOR

- ○ **POPULATION** 14.3 million
- ○ **FOREIGN VISITORS PER YEAR** 1.1 million
- ○ **CAPITAL** Quito
- ○ **LANGUAGES** Spanish, Quechua
- ○ **UNIT OF CURRENCY** US dollar ($)
- ○ **MAJOR INDUSTRIES** Oil, bananas
- ○ **COST INDEX** Bottle of Pilsener US$1.25, midrange hotel double/hostel dorm US$20/10, three-day Amazon excursion US$400

WHY GO IN 2013? MAKING TRACKS

There's a buzz in the Andean air of Ecuador this year – or, rather, a klaxon blast or three. The country's railway network, almost totally closed down in the years following the devastating El Niño–induced floods of the 1990s, is scheduled to radically revamp in 2013. A massive $250 million is rebuilding train lines between increasingly cosmopolitan Quito in the mountains and the coastal port of Guayaquil. Tracks will also connect Ecuador's famed 5900m-high volcano Cotopaxi and the Nariz del Diablo (Devil's Nose), claiming the steepest (and most hair-raising) stretch of railway in the Western world. Joining up these lofty locales by track wasn't easy – it's not for nothing that Ecuadorians dub their railway the most difficult train in the world – and the restoration has been Ecuador's most ambitious tourism project. But developers believe the gamble will pay off and pull in unprecedented tourist numbers.

And why wouldn't it? International visitors to this diminutive-yet-diverse South American nation are already at an all-time high and navigating it has never been so fun. And, in a more-or-less trackless continent, it's fun that no other country can come close to emulating. The highlight for travellers will be the opportunities to visit places they otherwise wouldn't: Machachi, with Ecuador's finest old haciendas, or the poignant archaeological site of Baños del Inca.

So: full steam ahead Ecuador. But if trains don't do it for you, chocolate will (logically, right?). The country produces some 60% of the world's quality cacao, and new, exclusively chocolate-themed tours of Ecuador kicked off in November 2012, planting the country firmly on the radar of serious chocoholics. Ecuador's wildlife, of course, is why tourism here first started, but this year the newsflash is that eco-excursions just got flashier. Snazzy Mashpi Lodge now offers Ecuador's first 'boutique Amazon' experience, with a treetop gondola whooshing guests 2km through the rainforest canopy.

LIFE-CHANGING EXPERIENCES

Quito is a great place to start your Ecuadorian foray, with one of the largest intact colonial cores of any South American city. It's Unesco-listed too, along with the country's other mountain metropolis, Cuenca. Near Quito there's the continent's best handicrafts markets at Otavalo, and one of the world's highest, most active and dramatic volcanoes, Cotopaxi, amid superb hiking in the surrounding national park. If you only have time for one train ride, make it the most legendary: the Riobamba–Alausi–Sibambe rail ride has been wowing travellers for generations, thanks to the ridiculously sheer switchback descent around the Nariz del Diablo. But here's Ecuador's real lure: you can be in the high Andes one minute, and either in the Amazon jungle or on the beach a few hours later. No other country in the world can offer such starkly different regions in such close proximity, or with such accessibility between them. Descend from the mountains to soak up volcanically heated spas in beautiful Baños or for some birding, Amazon-style, in the world's most biodiverse spot.

FESTIVALS & EVENTS

✪ Otavalo's Fiesta del Yamor is a September celebration of harvest dating to Inca times: traditionally the sun god was offered copious amounts of Andean corn-fermented liquor *chicha* (aka yamor), which features prominently in festivities.

✪ In November's Fiesta de Mama Negra in Latacunga, costumed characters reflecting Latacunga's diverse heritage parade the streets. The show-stealing figure is the *mama negra* (black mother): a combo of the Virgin and African deities.

✪ Citizens of Quito go *loco* (mad) in the week preceding the anniversary of their city's founding on 6 December. Top billing at these Fiestas de Quito is one of Latin America's biggest bullfighting contests (lasting eight successive days).

HOT TOPIC OF THE DAY

As if cross-country trains weren't enough, it seems Quito will get its own metro system (due 2016). Construction started late 2012, and Ecuadorians looked on with a mixture of pride and scepticism: aware, perhaps, of the see-saw nature of their public transportation over the decades.

MOST BIZARRE SIGHT

Ecuador has cashed in on straddling the equator and built the photo-friendly Mitad del Mundo experience, supposedly smack-bang on the divide between the hemispheres. Never will you watch water run down a plughole with such awe as when you observe demonstrations of the coriolis effect (water drains in an anticlockwise direction north of the equator and clockwise south). The *actual* equatorial line, however, is disputed: some say it's up to 240m north of the current mark. The experiment, strangely, still seems to work...

by Luke Waterson

NORTH AMERICA

⊕ **SLOVAKIA**
EUROPE

ASIA

'Secreted in this landscape is Slovakia's greatest draw: its wonderfully preserved folk culture'

AUSTRALIA

#5

ADVENTURE | OFF-ROAD | CULTURE

SLOVAKIA

- ⊕ **POPULATION** 5.4 million
- ⊕ **FOREIGN VISITORS PER YEAR** 1.3 million (2010)
- ⊕ **CAPITAL** Bratislava
- ⊕ **LANGUAGES** Slovak, Hungarian, Roma, Czech
- ⊕ **UNIT OF CURRENCY** Euro (€)
- ⊕ **MAJOR INDUSTRIES** Car production, electrical engineering
- ⊕ **COST INDEX** Slovak-brewed beer 500ml €1.50 (US$2), midrange hotel double/dorm €75/12 (US$98/16), train ticket Bratislava–Kosice €55 (US$70)

WHY GO IN 2013?
COUNTRY OF CULTURE

Happy 20th birthday, Slovakia. Two decades on from the Velvet Revolution that saw the country separate from its Czech neighbour, it has galvanised to form one of the continent's fastest-growing economies, joined the EU and ranks right up there in Google searches for bargain ski packages and stag weekends. Signs of capitalist success? Maybe. But Slovakia's economic boom has hampered visitor numbers (it's now too pricey for many Eastern Europeans who once visited) and Slovakia's tourism industry is keen to distance the nation from being all cheap pistes and piss-ups (they're not keen on overplaying the communist past either).

The image overhaul has been overdue but it's here, and in time for the inevitable party in 2013. Slovakia *has* come a long way, but the message now is that visitors could and should go a lot further into it. Slovakia's ski centres are looking spruced-up of recent years, but snow-sports are merely the gateway to a host of high-altitude activities in this mountainous land, like tracking some of Europe's last major wolf populations, just as Bratislava beer-bingeing can be traded for tasting Slovak wines in timeless villages that resound to ancient Romany or folk music. In the lower lands, Kosice is 2013 European

City of Culture, and will offer a scintillating program of film, folk, music, arts and crafts festivals across atmospheric locations such as its castle and restored amphitheatre.

Cruising along (or staying on) the Danube is getting bigger and more luxurious than ever. It's on this illustrious river, incidentally, that you'll find one of Eastern Europe's most magnificent waterside transformation projects: the Danubiana Meulensteen art museum, undoubtedly one of the region's greatest contemporary arts museums. Sorry, that should be *Central* Europe: that's the term Slovakians prefer nowadays. 'Eastern' is so eighties.

LIFE-CHANGING EXPERIENCES

It seems strange for a country so close to the hub of Europe, but Slovakia's commonly known parts are so sparse that travelling virtually anywhere is an adventure: as befits a nation more dominated by mountains or forests than almost any other on the continent. After sampling Bratislava's medieval Old Town and quirky communist architecture (some of the most distinctive behind the old Iron Curtain), head for the Tatras Mountains. Classic skiing at a fraction of Alpine prices awaits at resorts like Jasná, but hiking is first-class too: taking to the trails of national parks like Poloniny with its ancient beech forests, or Slovenský raj with its precarious cliff-scaling paths, is as remote as Europe gets, and a nigh-on primordial experience. Secreted in this landscape is Slovakia's greatest draw: its wonderfully preserved folk culture, the colourful roots of which are interlinked with the Romany heritage hereabouts. Roll back the centuries by stepping into one of Eastern

DON'T MISS THE DANUBIANA
MEULENSTEEN ART MUSEUM

Slovakia's wooden churches, or tapping into a folk festival at a venue like scenically set Východná. The former Czechoslovakia was Europe's most castellated region and Slovakia's share comprises some phenomenal fortresses: from moody Devín, overlooking the Danube, to Spiš, one of the continent's largest castles.

FESTIVALS & EVENTS

✪ Of all Slovakia's foodstuffs, *bryndza* (Slovak sheep's cheese) is among the most unique, enjoying EU protection of origin. Celebrate this in June at the Stoličné Dni, a 15th century-style Slovak market taking over Liptovský Mikuláš, with locally

produced traditional foods like *bryndza* showcased alongside folk acts.

✪ In June/July, Folklórny Festival Východná (Východná Folk Festival) erupts in the homonymous town: it's the biggest celebration of Slovak folk culture... anywhere.

✪ In early October, White Night transforms Kosice into an open-air gallery, with all manner of pioneering arty installations displayed on the streets; in 2013 it's one of the city's myriad cultural extravaganzas.

WHAT'S HOT...
Danube cruises, eco-excursions in the Tatras, Rom-pop (Romany pop music), ice hockey (still)

...WHAT'S NOT
Communist chants and the Quentin Tarantino-produced film *Hostel* (it portrayed Slovakia rife with people-trafficking, loose women and murder)

MOST BIZARRE SIGHT
Plenty of Bratislava's communist architecture qualifies as odd (an upside-down pyramid or Europe's biggest socialist housing development, anyone?) but the Nový Most (New Bridge), with its UFO-like restaurant/viewpoint/nightclub perched high above, has to be as close to the Space Age as a building on the Danube comes.

by Tony Wheeler

'These islands are laid back, friendly and often surprisingly untouched'

SOLOMON ISLANDS ⊙

#6

SOLOMON ISLANDS

- ⊙ **POPULATION** 538,000
- ⊙ **FOREIGN VISITORS PER YEAR** 20,000
- ⊙ **CAPITAL** Honiara
- ⊙ **LANGUAGES** Solomons Pijin and 74 indigenous languages, English is widely spoken.
- ⊙ **MAJOR INDUSTRIES** Subsistence farming and fishing, timber
- ⊙ **UNIT OF CURRENCY** Solomon Islands dollar (S$)
- ⊙ **COST INDEX** Bottle of Solbrew beer S$15 (US$2.50), night at a village homestay S$100-200 (US$15-30), a place with electricity and mod cons S$500-1500 (US$80-250), beautiful carved coconut wood bowl S$200-500 (US$30-80)

WHY GO 2013? EVENTUALLY THE OUTSIDE WORLD WILL WAKE UP TO THESE ISLANDS

Forget what travelling the Pacific *used* to be like – around the Solomon Islands it's still that way. These islands are laid back, friendly and often surprisingly untouched. This is not the Pacific of mass-market resorts or of luxury retreats; you're definitely not tripping over other visitors. What you will find is engaging eco-resorts, village homestays and some of the best scuba diving anywhere.

The Pacific theatre of WWII was never fought more fiercely than in the Solomons, and wartime descriptions like 'The Slot' and 'Iron Bottom Sound' have endured on modern maps. Wartime history can be traced around the battlefields of Guadalcanal and the rusting wreckage in the jungle. At Fatboys Resort just outside Ghizo you can take a kayak and paddle out to Kennedy Island: yes, that's where JFK, 20 years before he became US president, swam to after his PT 109 patrol boat was T-boned by a Japanese destroyer.

But you need scuba gear for the real excitement. There's everything from ditched US fighter aircraft to sunken Japanese cargo ships for divers to explore and the water is so warm you don't even need a wetsuit. 'I'm a Solomons boy', one divemaster said. 'When the temperature drops below 30°C I shiver.'

Even flying in to Honiara, the capital, is a reminder that the Solomons are well back in the development rankings. You fly over an awful lot of untouched jungle and towering mountains as you cross the island from the southern Weathercoast. It's an early indicator that this is a great destination if jungle trekking, volcano climbing, ocean kayaking and even surfing are on your must-do lists. Birdwatching is right up there as well; the bird list is long and colourful and some of the islands are so remote that new species are still turning up. Don't miss the local crafts either – the islanders turn out some of the Pacific's most beautiful wooden bowls, often inlaid with shells.

In the past limited flights, difficult internal transport, a lack of infrastructure, a nasty little local civil war and some particularly exotic strains of malaria all put travellers off. Today travel is much easier, the civil strife is off the radar and lately even the mosquitoes aren't so threatening, although you should still pack your insect repellent and take those antimalarials.

LIFE-CHANGING EXPERIENCES

With nearly 1000 islands scattered over nearly 1000km from northwest to southeast the old line that 'getting there is half the fun' is bound to come in to play. Flights touch down on grass airstrips where the terminal is a hut, you do your own baggage handling and dogs have to be chased off the runway before you can take off. The lineup of inter-island vessels at Honiara's town-centre dock clearly put the tramp into 'tramp steamer'. Safety may not be their number-one feature, but they can certainly make travel an adventure. At some point you may find yourself in a smaller boat, out at sea with water splashing over you and that trusty outboard buzzing in the background.

FESTIVALS & EVENTS

✪ The missionaries had a huge influence on the Solomons and many holidays come from the Christian calendar, particularly Whit Monday in May/June with marching, dancing and singing on many islands.
✪ Every province has its own regional festival, scattered right across the year.

RECENT FAD

Internet connections, mobile phones and ATMs. Internet cafes are popping up and a 'Bumblebee card' lets you log on to wi-fi networks with your own laptop. Mobile-phone coverage is arriving in more island centres and ATMs are no longer restricted to just two banks in the capital city.

HOT TOPIC OF THE DAY

Flying to the Solomons is getting easier; at one time Solomon Airlines managed to acquire a plane which couldn't fly to the country carrying both passengers and their baggage. Now there's a choice of connections to Australia and other neighbouring countries.

MOST BIZARRE SIGHT

Uepi Island Resort's 'Welcome Wharf' is also home to the island's 'welcome sharks' which seem to be on constant patrol. 'It's the best snorkelling spot on the island', you're told on arrival. Followed by, 'oh they're quite friendly'.

A TRADITIONAL DANCE WITH
A WAR CLUB, TIKOPIA ISLAND,
THE SOLOMONS

by Brandon Presser

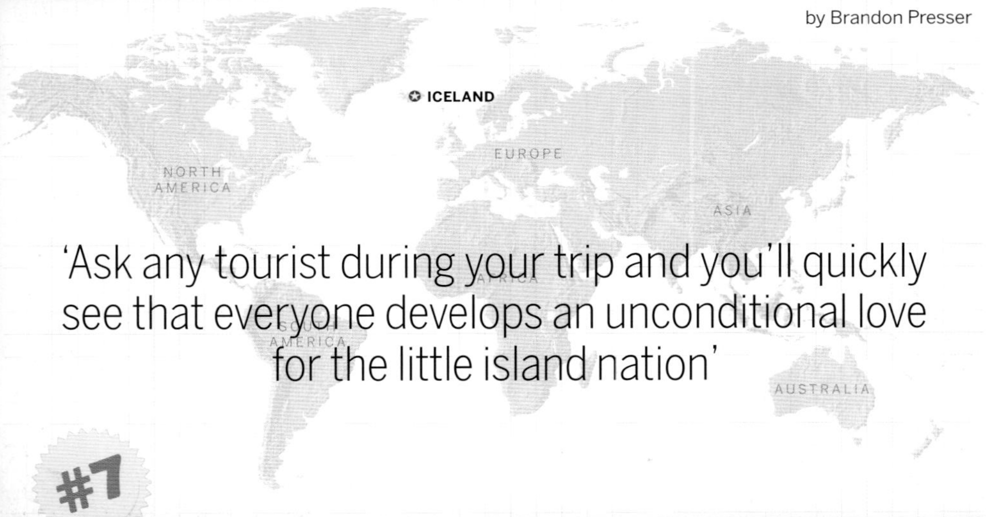

○ ICELAND

NORTH AMERICA

EUROPE

ASIA

AUSTRALIA

'Ask any tourist during your trip and you'll quickly see that everyone develops an unconditional love for the little island nation'

#7

ACTIVITIES | OFF-ROAD | VALUE

ICELAND

- ✪ **POPULATION** 318,452
- ✪ **FOREIGN VISITORS PER YEAR** 495,000
- ✪ **CAPITAL** Reykjavik
- ✪ **LANGUAGES** Icelandic, English
- ✪ **MAJOR INDUSTRIES** Fisheries, tourism
- ✪ **UNIT OF CURRENCY** Icelandic króna (ISK)
- ✪ **COST INDEX** Cup of coffee ISK350 (US$2.74), dorm bed per night ISK4400 (US$35), car rental per day ISK14,300 (US$117), hotel internet access free, *hlollar bàtar* sandwich ISK790 (US$6)

WHY GO IN 2013? LAST CHANCE TO BEAT THE CROWDS

Iceland is a land of strange phenomena – volcanoes spew molten ash, streamers of fluorescence dance in the winter sky, and hidden elves are commonly believed to lurk between the stone-strewn fjords. But perhaps the most striking thing about the country is the devotion it inspires among its visitors. Ask any tourist during your trip and you'll quickly see that everyone develops an unconditional love for the little island nation, whether it's for the mind-bending scenery that crops up in every direction, the platefuls of delicious lamb and fish dishes, or the sincere local hospitality cloaked under the gruff Nordic welcome.

Tales of deeply personal adventures spread like wildfire upon one's homecoming, which has, in the last five years, encouraged an exponential increase in visitors. The currency crash – which effectively devalued the króna by 75% – also helped make a trip to Iceland much more favourable to the wallet. But now, as the global economy starts to heal, prices are climbing once more.

The spoils of Iceland are no longer a secret, but they're still yours for the taking – and in 2013 you'll still be well ahead of the curve, as there are plenty of rugged nooks and crannies left to explore.

LIFE-CHANGING EXPERIENCES

Tackling the so-called Ring Road is a must for all travellers: it will reveal Iceland as oh-so-much more than a land of ice. Follow the path anticlockwise, taking in the coloured

INTREPID EXPLORER LEIF ERIKSSON STANDS BEFORE HALLGRIMSKIRKJA CHURCH, REYKJAVIK

sands and notorious volcanoes of the southern coast before rounding up the east to enjoy fishermen's hamlets and tucked-away puffin colonies. Check out the marshy plains of the northeast, the mysterious lake at Myvatn, and the myriad waterfalls of the northwest, then round back towards the capital, stopping in to see the misty cliffs and hidden cairns along the Snaefellsness peninsula – said to be one of the earth's energy centres. If time permits, take a detour to the far-flung Westfjords region, which looks like lobster claws clipping away at the Arctic Circle – it's here that you'll find the country's most dramatic iteration of thin, deep bays; the home of resting whales.

FESTIVALS & EVENTS

✪ On 17 June the country's largest festival commemorates the founding of the Republic of Iceland in 1944 with parades and general merriment. Tradition has it that the sun isn't supposed to shine. And it usually doesn't!

✪ Iceland Airwaves started in 1999 as a bunch of DJs scratching records, and today it's grown to epic proportions, attracting the likes of Robyn and Fat Boy Slim – suddenly the weather-variable month of October is one of the best times to visit!

WHAT'S HOT...

Eating *hàkarl*. Adventurous eaters looking to dare their taste buds should try *hàkarl* – rotten Greenland shark (tastes like old cheese dipped in ammonia). Yum.

...WHAT'S NOT

Eating whale. Iceland's whaling laws are contentious on the world stage; besides, there are other things to try in Iceland's Hall of Horrors (aka the kitchen).

RANDOM FACTS

✪ Iceland has the highest density of mobile-phone use in the world – there are more phones in use than there are people.

✪ Beer was illegal in Iceland until 1989. In an attempt to circumvent the law, several Reykjavik pubs served nonalcoholic beer mixed with vodka.

✪ Iceland publishes the greatest number of books per capita in the world, and the literacy rate is a perfect 100%.

✪ During the filming of *Dancer in the Dark*, director Lars von Trier was supposedly so brutal to Icelandic singer Björk that he drove her to the brink of sanity – she apparently ate her own cardigan.

MOST BIZARRE SIGHT

The Inuit thought they were the souls of the dead, Scandinavian folklore described them as the spirits of unmarried women, and the Japanese believed that a child conceived under the dancing rays would be fortunate in life. Modern science, however, has a very different take on the Northern Lights, or *aurora borealis*: the magical curtains of colour that streak across the northern night sky are the result of solar wind – a stream of particles from the sun that collides with oxygen, nitrogen and hydrogen in the upper atmosphere. These collisions produce the haunting greens and magentas as the earth's magnetic field draws the wind towards the polar regions.

The best time to see the Northern Lights in Iceland is on a clear night between September and April.

by Brett Atkinson

NORTH AMERICA

EUROPE

✪ TURKEY

ASIA

AUSTRALIA

'Breakfast of local honey, freshly baked flatbread, cheese and yoghurt from your host family's sheep should make the tourist buzz seem very far way'

OFF-ROAD | CULTURE | FOOD

TURKEY

- ✪ **POPULATION** 79 million
- ✪ **FOREIGN VISITORS PER YEAR** 32 million
- ✪ **CAPITAL** Ankara
- ✪ **LANGUAGES** Turkish, Kurdish (unofficial)
- ✪ **MAJOR INDUSTRIES** Tourism, textiles, petroleum
- ✪ **UNIT OF CURRENCY** Turkish Lira (TL)
- ✪ **COST INDEX** *Lahmacun* (Turkish pizza) in Gaziantep TL5 (US$2.50), bottle of Efes beer TL8 (US$4.50), boutique hotel room in Mardin TL200 (US$110), entrance to Gaziantep's Zeugma Mosaics Museum TL5 (US$2.50)

WHY GO IN 2013?
EASTERN PROMISES

OK, maybe you've already been to Turkey, but have you *really seen* Turkey? Plan a return visit to venture southeast and discover Turkey beyond Istanbul and the coastal resorts. New low-cost airlines conveniently link the region to Istanbul, and excellent bus services make getting around easy.

The honey-coloured old towns of Mardin and Midyat showcase boutique hotels in heritage Ottoman mansions, and terrace teahouses feature views across the Plains of Mesopotamia. Gaziantep's culinary firepower is renowned across the country, and the city's superb new Zeugma Mosaics Museum features astounding works of art including the poignant Roman-era *Gypsy Girl*.

Significantly older are the recently uncovered ruins of Göbekli Tepe near Sanliurfa. Predating Stonehenge by 6000 years, the 12,000-year-old Neolithic structure is reckoned to be the world's oldest temple. The slow, but scenic, way to reach Göbekli Tepe is on the recently inaugurated Abraham's Path walking trail. The trekking route begins in Harran, the nearby birthplace of the prophet Abraham, before continuing on through Syria, Jordan, the West Bank and Israel.

Accommodation on some parts of the path's meandering route through southeastern Turkey's sun-baked Biblical landscape is in simple Kurdish homestays. A breakfast of local honey, freshly baked flatbread, and cheese and yoghurt from your host family's fat-tailed sheep will make the coast's tourist buzz or Istanbul's Old Town seem far way. Welcome to the real Turkey.

LIFE-CHANGING EXPERIENCES

Ferry-hop between Europe and Asia on the bustling Bosphorus before extending your seaborne explorations to include the sleepy Princes Islands. Tease your taste buds with a tour of Istanbul's markets, and then learn the secrets of Turkish cuisine at a cookery class. Further east in Anatolia, experience the echoes of past civilisations amid the poignant remains of Ani and Afrodisias.

FESTIVALS & EVENTS

✪ One year after the London Olympics the mightiest of the Med's athletes will descend on Mersin for June's Mediterranean Games. Turkey's fourth on the all-time medal ladder, so factor in 2013's home advantage and prospects are good.

✪ Late June sees *pehlivan* (wrestlers) from around Turkey grapple with other slippery olive-oil-slathered sportsmen at the annual Kirkpinar Oil Wrestling Festival in the western city of Edirne.

✪ For two months from mid-September 2013, the 13th International Istanbul Biennial will further cement the city's reputation as one of the planet's hip hubs for visual arts.

RECENT FAD

Regional cuisine from eastern Turkey is becoming popular in Istanbul. Catch a ferry across the Bosphorus to Kadikoy for Ciya Sofrasi's spin on eastern Anatolia's collage of Levantine and Arab flavours. In the hip suburb of Cihangir, the Van Kahvalti Evi (Van

Breakfast House) specialises in the feasts of the eastern city of Van. Tuck into herb-studded cheeses, *kaymak* (clotted cream) with honey, and *menemen* (scrambled eggs) for the ultimate kick-start to the day.

HOT TOPIC OF THE DAY

Many regional Turkish cities are investing in new museums. Leading the way is the southeastern city of Gaziantep where the superb Zeugma Mosaics Museum is complemented by excellent exhibitions of Turkish ethnography and cuisine. The city is also planning a new museum to feature the history of traditional Turkish bath houses.

RANDOM FACTS

✪ Baklava is famed from Bosnia to Lebanon, but the world's finest alchemy of gossamer-thin filo pastry, chopped pistachios and syrup comes from Gaziantep.

✪ Coffee was introduced to European society following 1683's Battle of Vienna between the Ottoman and Holy Roman Empires. Reputedly, bags of the fragrant beans were found discovered in abandoned Ottoman military camps.

✪ Pure-white Van cats from the eastern city of Van often have eyes of two different colours. They also love to swim – handy when you live around Turkey's largest lake.

MOST BIZARRE SIGHT

Explore Cappadocia's honeycombed landscape of wind-eroded volcanic *tufa* by hot-air balloon, horseback, or on your own two legs. Central Anatolia's premier tourist destination is now wildly popular, but it's still easy for intrepid travellers to escape deeper into the region's quirky moonscape labyrinth.

by Leslie Davisson

○ DOMINICAN REPUBLIC

'It's as if someone took a look at your wishlist and purpose-built the perfect vacation destination'

#9

ADVENTURE | VALUE | EVENTS

DOMINICAN REPUBLIC

- ○ **POPULATION** 10 million
- ○ **FOREIGN VISITORS PER YEAR** 4.2 million
- ○ **CAPITAL** Santo Domingo
- ○ **LANGUAGE** Spanish
- ○ **MAJOR INDUSTRIES** Sugar, tourism
- ○ **UNIT OF CURRENCY** Dominican Republic peso (RD$)
- ○ **COST INDEX** Bottle of Presidente beer RD$50 (US$1.30), overnight stay in midrange hotel in Punta Cana RD$3500 (US$90), one-hour merengue lesson RD$250 (US$6.50)

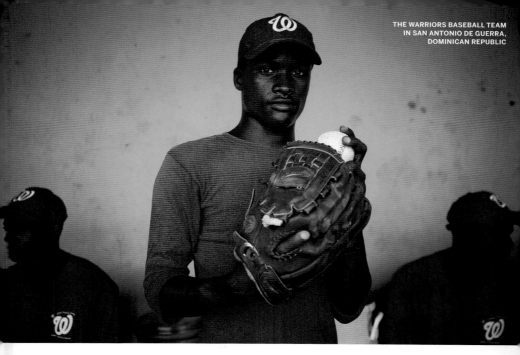

WHY GO IN 2013? GET THERE BEFORE EVERYONE ELSE DOES

There is a reason Columbus landed here first. Travelling to the Dominican Republic ('the DR') now is akin to seeing a great new band in a small club before they start playing arena shows. But people are catching on: in the first quarter of 2012 the Dominican Republic saw an 8.4% increase in tourism. With more airlines offering stops to the country's eight international airports, as well as cruise ships adding the DR as a major port of call, more people are escaping to the land of sun, sand and surf. In preparation for this new wave of visitors, a large number of new hotels and resorts are set to open their doors in 2013. Relatively untouched by the devastating 2010 earthquake in neighbouring Haiti, the country has major infrastructure development underway, including road construction, to make it even easier to spend more time on the beach and less time getting there.

So now that the secret is out, we can share why the DR is on our hit parade. It's as if someone took a look at your wishlist and purpose-built the perfect vacation destination. Sip a cocktail made from local rum while you watch the whales swim by. Own the dance floor with salsa and merengue lessons. Brave the rapids in the only raftable river in the Caribbean. This small but mighty country boasts plenty of action for the adventurer in you, as well as 400km of coastline to help you get in touch

with your inner beach bum. The warm climate is year-round and, unlike many other tropical getaways, the Dominican Republic is still relatively affordable. As if it needed any more going for it, how about adding friendly locals who are always ready to share a smile, a beer and a story?

But scratch the sun-soaked surface of the DR and you will find a destination that exudes culture, including a rich history of music and dance (it's the birthplace of merengue), a proud legacy of sports heroes, and influential art galleries and museums.

LIFE-CHANGING EXPERIENCE

Hike, climb and swim your way up the 27 waterfalls of Damajagua. Once you have made your way to the top of mountain the only way down is to slip, slide and jump into the waters below. Some of the leaps are 10m high. And yes, you are handed a helmet and a life preserver at the beginning of the journey, but don't give it a second thought. The journey is a test of will that will make you feel like a true bad-ass explorer once you splash down into the final pool of water.

FESTIVALS & EVENTS

✪ Carnival is celebrated all month long in February, and each weekend the streets are filled with costumes and parades. The final blow-out fiesta is held the last weekend in February. It's a raucous dance party, street festival and heated costume competition all rolled into one.

✪ Who needs to spend money on big-league baseball tickets and overpriced beer when you can have the same experience in the ballparks of the DR? The country's

leading players compete for the top spot during the winter months, ending with the championship series in January.

✪ A giant birthday party for the merengue, the Puerto Plata Merengue Festival lasts three days in October and is filled with local food, arts and crafts, and of course, musicians and dancers. The streets are closed off to traffic, allowing for maximum room for sultry dance moves.

WHAT'S HOT...

Coffee-tourism, ecotourism, baseball (always)

...WHAT'S NOT

Bribery scandals, misinformation about damage from the 2010 earthquake

HOT TOPIC OF THE DAY

Roads. Yes, roads. The newly opened Coral Highway is a fast and modern link between two major destinations: Punta Cana and the capital city Santo Domingo. The road takes drivers along a gorgeous stretch beside beaches and small fishing villages.

RANDOM FACTS

✪ The Dominican Republic has provided the second-largest number of players to Major League Baseball (after the US).

✪ Forget finding a bar or nightclub. For locals, the place to party is the car wash. Yup, suds mixed with Presidente beer, music and dancing.

✪ Nelson de la Rosa was not only a native of the DR and an actor, he was one of the shortest men in the world, measuring just 71cm. You can spot him opposite Marlon Brando in the film *The Island of Dr Moreau*.

by Jean-Bernard Carillet

'Prepare to be overwhelmed: in both fauna and landscapes, the world's fourth-biggest island is otherworldly'

○ MADAGASCAR

#10

ACTIVITIES | ADVENTURE | OFF-ROAD

MADAGASCAR

- ○ **POPULATION** 21 million
- ○ **FOREIGN VISITORS PER YEAR** 225,000
- ○ **CAPITAL** Antananarivo
- ○ **LANGUAGES** French, Malagasy
- ○ **MAJOR INDUSTRIES** Agriculture, tourism
- ○ **UNIT OF CURRENCY** Ariary (Ar)
- ○ **COST INDEX** Ice-cold THB beer Ar2000 (US$0.92), single dive Ar100,000 (US$46), double in a midrange hotel in Antananarivo from Ar80,000 (US$37), catch-of-the-day fish Ar12,000 (US$5.50)

RING-TAILED LEMURS ARE
NATIVE TO MADAGASCAR

WHY GO IN 2013? A WORLD OF WILD WONDERS

After years of political instability and uncertainty, which has hampered tourism development, Madagascar is on the verge of recovery. In 2013, expect a fresh wind of change with a move towards greater democracy following presidential elections. For visitors, the time to go is now, before the country reappears in travel agents' windows. Be prepared to be overwhelmed: in both fauna and landscapes, the world's fourth-biggest island is otherworldly. When Madagascar slipped away from the ancient megacontinent of Gondwana some 90 million years ago, its cargo of primitive animals was pushed and pulled by evolutionary forces into myriad shapes and sizes. Today, more than 80% of the wildlife inhabiting this 1600km-long territory is unique to Madagascar. It's an African country with a unique twist. No elephants, lions or hyenas here, but an array of quirky species found nowhere else on earth: lemurs, tenrecs, fossas, chameleons and jabadys, among others. The undisputed stars are lemurs (more than 50 species!), especially the diademed sifaka and the

indri, which are great fun to observe. Small wonder that for a good number of visitors, this Noah's Ark in the Indian Ocean is synonymous with wildlife-watching and ecotourism. Good news: most species can be approached with relative ease, and a large number of national parks and reserves ensure that they're protected.

The scenery is almost as surreal and stimulating as the exotic wildlife: high plateaus that plunge into semitropical rainforest, mangrove swamps, volcanic craters, uninhabited offshore islands, beautiful untouched beaches, dry hills in all shades of brown, pristine coral reefs and grandiose mountain ranges. The whole country is pockmarked with trippy natural attractions, such as the Avenue du Baobab, which features a line of giant trees more than one thousand years old. To those seeking paradise lost and a place out of the ordinary, Madagascar cannot fail to delight. Just don't forget your adventurer's hat!

LIFE-CHANGING EXPERIENCES

If you're in search of unforgettable memories, plan several days of hiking in the

A LOCAL WOMAN PASSES BAOBAB TREES IN MORONDAVA, TOLIARA, MADAGASCAR

ceremonies take place every year between June and September in the highlands region from Antananarivo south to Ambositra.

✪ You can attend circumcision festivals held by most tribes between June and September, and in November and December in the southwest.

✪ If you're after something light-hearted, make a beeline for the Santabary in April and May – it's the first rice harvest.

RANDOM FACTS

✪ Air Madagascar, the national carrier once officially called Madair and now known affectionately as Airmad, has never suffered a crash.

✪ Madagascar has the world's smallest chameleon – the pygmy leaf chameleon – which is smaller than your thumb. It resembles a dead leaf.

✪ When drinking in Madagascar, it's customary to pour a little on the ground first as an offering to the ancestors.

✪ Presumably a legacy of the French, cakes, croissants, pastries and baguettes are on sale in even the most humble of cafes.

MOST BIZARRE SIGHT

The *tsingy*! These pointy, limestone pinnacles that seem to soar like missiles from the ground were sharpened to razor edges by the movement of wind and water over centuries and are Madagascar's most striking attraction. They often reach several hundred metres in height. Walkways and bridges allow visitors to climb on top of the smaller areas of *tsingy*. The most impressive *tsingy* are within the Parc National des Tsingy de Bemaraha.

Parc National de l'Isalo. The geography of this vast national park is mind-blowing, with a mix of canyons, plains, cliffs, waterfalls and colourful mountain ranges made of eroded Jurassic sandstone. It also offers superb wildlife-viewing opportunities – you're sure to see several bizarre species of lemurs, including sifaka and ringtail lemurs.

FESTIVALS & EVENTS

✪ Among the most unusual Malagasy ceremonies are the Famadihana (literally the 'turning of the bones'). These reburial

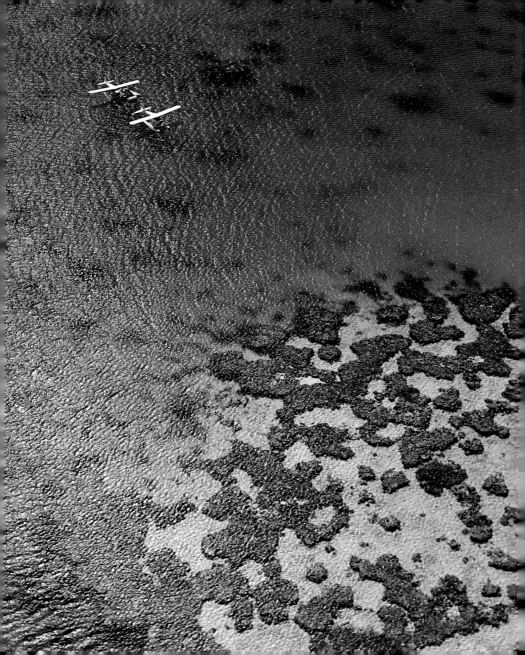

LONELY PLANET'S

TOP 10

REGIONS

by Abigail Blasi

NORTH
AMERICA

EUROPE

⊙ **CORSICA**

ASIA

AFRICA

AMERICA

AUSTRALIA

'It's this epic beauty combined with the challenging topography that makes it a spectacular choice to host the historic centenary of the Tour de France'

#1

🏃 ACTIVITIES | 🎆 EVENTS | 🍴 FOOD

CORSICA, FRANCE

- ⊙ **POPULATION** 260,000
- ⊙ **MAIN TOWNS** Ajaccio, Bastia
- ⊙ **LANGUAGES** French, Corsican, Italian
- ⊙ **MAJOR INDUSTRY** Tourism
- ⊙ **UNIT OF CURRENCY** Euro (€)
- ⊙ **COST INDEX** Glass of beer €2.50 (US$3.30), hotel double for a night €80-300 (US$100-30), short taxi ride €10 (US$13), diving session from €50 (US$65)

SCANDOLA NATURE RESERVE, CORSICA, FRANCE

WHY GO IN 2013? THE CENTENARY OF THE TOUR DE FRANCE

Mixing the cultures of Italy and France yet remaining fiercely Corsican, the French Mediterranean island of Corsica has a furious beauty. Its mountainous interior is carpeted in jade-green *maquis* (scrub), which scents the air with wild herbs and equals the blue sky in the intensity of colour. The greenery runs all the way down to the blinding white sands of the beaches, and in springtime is dotted with floral colour: poppy reds and delicate violet. It's this epic beauty combined with the challenging topography that makes it a spectacular choice to host the historic centenary of the Tour de France.

Race organisers wanted the hundredth Tour to have an enchanting and spectacular location, and decided Corsica was the place; this will be the first time the race has braved its challenges. The island will host the first three stages: first is Porto Vecchio to Bastia (201.5km), a beautiful coastal route, with an exciting sprint finish. Bastia to Ajaccio (153km) crosses Corsica's vertiginous interior, and involves some intense climbs, such as that over the Col de Vizzavona pass. The final stretch is another mountainous stage from Ajaccio to Calvi (145km), offering mesmerising views over the pink-red rock formations around Piana to the northwest. And if you're wondering why the race, created by French rider and sports journalist Henri Desgrange in 1903, marks its centenary this year, it's because it did not take place during the two World Wars.

LIFE-CHANGING EXPERIENCES

With no vehicle access or footpath, you'll have to get to the beautiful, protected Réserve Naturelle de Scandola, to the west of the island, by sea. Here golden-red rocks meet the saturated turquoise of the sea in an extraordinary marriage of colour. Corsica's rocky, green interior also offers some unforgettable landscapes and challenges, including the world-famous GR20, a long-distance walking route, which can be done in its entirety in two weeks or in more manageable sections.

FESTIVALS & EVENTS

◐ Every July, the small village of Patrimonio hosts the *Nuits de la Guitare*, a music festival at which previous headliners have included Tom Jones and Iggy and the Stooges.
◐ The Festival d'Erbalunga is another excellent music festival in a small town, which takes place in August, and makes use of Brando's small amphitheatre.

HOT TOPIC OF THE DAY

The centenary of the Tour de France, the world's most famous cycle race, in cycling-mad Corsica is definitely *the* talking point of 2013.

RANDOM FACTS

◐ No part of Corsica is more than 42km from the sea.
◐ It's said that Ulysses and his men took shelter in Bonifacio's cliff-shadowed port, where they met with a race of giants.
◐ During his education in France, Corsica's most famous son, Napoleon, was mercilessly teased for his Corsican accent.

◐ The *maquis* (shrub) consists of more than 2000 different species of plants and flowers, 78 of which are unique to Corsica.

MOST BIZARRE SIGHT

Menhirs with carved faces at Filitosa, south of Ajaccio: these haunting faces peering out from the rock date from 1500 BC.

DEFINING DIFFERENCE

Due to its prime position in the Mediterranean, Corsica has been invaded by the Romans, Vandals, Ostrogoths, Byzantines, Saracens, Aragons and Greeks, and was fought over by Italy and

France for centuries. The island had a short-lived period of independence from 1725 to 1807 before the French took over again, and since then Corsica has been officially part of France. Yet this magical island feels different from the mainland in everything from customs to cuisine, and its language and temperament are very distinct. The proud, austere Corsican character has long been epitomised by its historical devotion to the vendetta. This tradition of revenge over matters of honour claimed many lives during the 17th and 18th centuries, and still resonates today – so, whatever you do, do not cross a Corsican.

REGIONAL FLAVOURS

Corsica is famous for its delicious charcuterie, with a delectable array of cured meats bulging out of its specialist shops. The distinctive, aromatic flavours arise from the fact that Corsican pigs are free to roam, and feed on chestnuts. Look out for *prisuttu* (dry ham), *lonzu* (tender smoked fillet), *coppa* (shoulder), *figatellu* (liver sausage), *salamu* (salami-style sausage), and *terrine de sanglier* (wild-boar pâté).

Local cheeses are also good, with glorious flavours and textures, from the hard, tangy *tomme corse* (semihard ewe's-milk cheese) to the king of the island's cheeses, *brocciu* (a crumbly white ewe's- or goat's-milk cheese).

by Dan Savery Raz

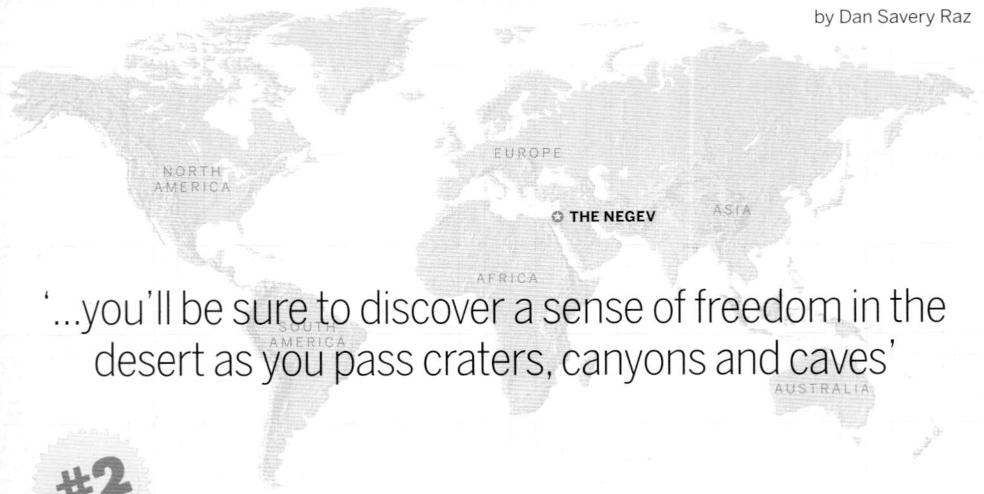

NORTH
AMERICA

EUROPE

○ **THE NEGEV**

ASIA

AFRICA

SOUTH
AMERICA

AUSTRALIA

'...you'll be sure to discover a sense of freedom in the desert as you pass craters, canyons and caves'

#2

ACTIVITIES   ADVENTURE   OFF-ROAD

THE NEGEV, ISRAEL

- ○ **POPULATION** 630,000
- ○ **MAIN TOWN** Be'er Sheva
- ○ **LANGUAGES** Hebrew, Arabic, English
- ○ **MAJOR INDUSTRIES** Tourism, agriculture, greentech
- ○ **UNIT OF CURRENCY** New Israeli Shekel (NIS)
- ○ **COST INDEX** Double/dorm room in guesthouse 450/100NIS (US$120/27), *labaneh* (yoghurt cheese) and pita bread 20NIS (US$5.30), three-hour bus ride from Be'er Sheva to Eilat 55NIS (US$14), 90-minute camel ride 135NIS (US$36)

WHY GO IN 2013? A NEW LEASE OF LIFE

For decades the Negev was regarded as nothing but a desolate desert. But today this region is a giant greenhouse of development. Think eco-villages, spa resorts and wineries. Yes, wineries.

Thanks to computerised drip irrigation, the Negev Highlands now has its own wine route. A crop of 21st-century vineyards has been springing up south of the city of Be'er Sheva, offering a taste of the Napa Valley in the Negev.

The desert also provides the perfect environment to learn about water conservation and renewable energy, both important issues in 2013. The *kibbutzim* of Sde Boker, Lotan and Ketura all offer ecological workshops and the last is home to Israel's first solar field.

Then there's the Makhtesh Ramon crater, Israel's very own Grand Canyon. Last year the Mitzpe Ramon Visitors' Centre was reopened with a new astronomy museum and the surrounding lunar landscape is an atmospheric space to do some star-gazing.

But a bigger bang is coming. In the next few years a new international airport at Timna is scheduled to open, followed by a high-speed railway to Eilat and more hotels. Time is running out to experience the desert as nature intended.

LIFE-CHANGING EXPERIENCES

Whether you go off-road by 4WD, bicycle or

on foot, you'll be sure to discover a sense of freedom in the desert as you pass craters, canyons and caves. Get a taste of the ancient spice route at the Nabataean ruins of Avdat, Shivta and Mamshit, try a spot of Watsu (water shiatsu) at Kibbutz Lotan and take a dive at the colourful Red Sea reef. Explore the galaxy by star-gazing at Makhtesh Ramon, spot a wild ibex in the Ein Avdat National Park and witness migrating birds from Africa as they pass through the Arava valley, a great highway in the sky.

FESTIVALS & EVENTS

✪ Shake your money-maker as the International Belly Dance Festival comes to Eilat in January.

✪ Open your chakras with a yoga workshop at the Zorba Festival held at Ashram in the Desert, south of Mitzpe Ramon, on Passover (late March) and Sukkot (September).

✪ Cool it down after a day in the blazing desert sun at the Red Sea Jazz Festival held every August, with free outdoor jams at the Yam Suf Hotel on Eilat's Coral Beach.

WHAT'S HOT...

Solar heating, creative recycling, wine-tasting, Red Sea kite-surfing, birdwatching

...WHAT'S NOT

Nuclear testing, landfilling, water-wasting, Red Sea polluting, TV-watching

HOT TOPIC OF THE DAY

Refugees. The western Negev has become a frontline in the refugee debate. Every month more than a thousand Africans cross the Egyptian border into Israel. In 2012 the

A ROAD SKIRTS THE RIM OF MAKHTESH RAMON CRATER, NEGEV DESERT, ISRAEL

Israeli government approved a bill to build a detention centre in the Negev that could hold up to 10,000 people. The topic has split the nation, with some arguing that Israel cannot support an endless influx of people, while others believe that it has a duty to offer shelter to those fleeing persecution.

RANDOM FACTS

✪ The Negev makes up nearly 60% of Israel's landmass but is home to just 8% of the population.

✪ The ancient ruins of Avdat provided the backdrop for the 1973 film of Andrew Lloyd Webber's musical *Jesus Christ Superstar*.

✪ The Negev is home to around 160,000 Bedouin, half of whom are nomadic.

✪ The world's biggest curved solar dish (nicknamed PETAL) is at the Ben-Gurion National Solar Energy Centre in Sde Boker.

DEFINING DIFFERENCE

The Negev feels like a different planet, well away from the hustle and bustle of the rest of the country. The pace of life is so laid back that locals call it *zaman midbar* (desert time).

REGIONAL FLAVOURS

The harsh conditions of the Negev make surprisingly good terrain for mountain goats and there are a number of farms offering dairy delights. Kornmehl Farm near Sde Boker specialises in goat's-cheese platters, pizzas and yoghurts. Wherever you are in the Negev, you're never far from a plate of *labaneh* – yoghurt made from cheese, usually served with *za'atar* (hyssop herb), olives and pita bread. But for a real taste of the desert, try some Bedouin *maqloobeh* (upside-down chicken and rice), followed by the traditional three cups of mint tea or black coffee.

by Tony Wheeler

NORTH AMERICA

EUROPE

ASIA

○ MUSTANG, NEPAL

'Up here everything is sharp, severe and absolute: the colours are vivid, the terrain is rugged, the air is crisp...'

AUSTRALIA

#3

ADVENTURE   OFF-ROAD   CULTURE

MUSTANG, NEPAL

- ○ **POPULATION** 15,000
- ○ **MAIN TOWN** Lo Manthang
- ○ **LANGUAGES** Tibetan, Nepalese
- ○ **MAJOR INDUSTRIES** Trade, apples, tourism
- ○ **UNIT OF CURRENCY** Nepalese rupee (Rs)
- ○ **COST INDEX** Nepal government trekking permit for Mustang US$500, hot shower at a village guest house Rs100 (US$1.25), a cutthroat razor shave in a Pokhara barber after the trek Rs100 (US$1.25)

WHY GO 2013? SEE THE FORBIDDEN KINGDOM BEFORE THE ROAD CHANGES IT FOREVER

Only a few years ago it was 'nobody's been there', now it's heading towards 'last chance to see'. The completion of a road connecting Mustang to China in the north and the rest of Nepal to the south will make all the difference. Lo Manthang, or Mustang as it's usually called, has been dubbed 'little Tibet' or 'the last forbidden kingdom'. Politically part of Nepal, in language, culture, climate and geography, it's Tibet. The remote region is north of the Himalayan watershed and on the Tibetan plateau, and just south of the border with 'big Tibet', the Chinese one.

Until 1992 nobody from outside was allowed in; for a while after that it was opened up to a few hundred a year, and these days anyone can enter, though the pricey trekking permit keeps the numbers down. There's also a restricted season for visits: in winter it's too cold and the snow too deep, so for months each year it again becomes a 'forbidden kingdom'. Much of the population heads south to India and further afield during these winter months to exercise their legendary trading abilities.

Up here everything is sharp, severe and absolute: the colours are vivid, the terrain is rugged, the air is crisp; it's either desert-dry or river-rapids, sere and barren or a flash of irrigated green.

LIFE-CHANGING EXPERIENCES

From the moment you enter the restricted Mustang region at Kagbeni you're in a different world. Villages are medieval and often focused on the monastery; Lo Manthang is a walled town where you feel

the main gate could still be slammed shut nightly. This is a place where until recently the wheel was used for spinning prayers, not providing transport, and you'll still meet horse and mule trains carrying goods and people along the trails. As you hike, look for the monastic cave retreats pockmarking sheer cliff faces – you might catch a glimpse of a monk looking out from one, as retreats still form part of religious life. Keep your eyes open for snow leopards on the remote trails (you'll certainly see moth-eaten, stuffed ones in some of the monastery gompas). But yaks, at high altitudes, and blue sheep, if you're lucky, are much more likely.

FESTIVALS & EVENTS

✪ Around May, Tiji (or Tenche) marks the end of winter and the start of spring with colourful dances, the burning of a demon figure and explosive musket fire.

✪ The Yartung festival in late August features parades, horse races and the consumption of large quantities of *chhang* (barley beer).

RECENT FADS

Technology is the big story these days, whether it's solar water heating, solar power panels, the solar kettle (like a shiny satellite dish that focusses the sun's rays on a kettle), real satellite dishes or mobile phones. There's even internet connection in Kagbeni, the entry point to the Mustang region, and in Lo Manthang itself. Guesthouses are popping up along the trekking trail, opening the route to independent trekkers, not just for organised treks carrying camping equipment. Kagbeni even features a YakDonalds, although surprisingly there's no Big Yak on the menu.

HOT TOPIC OF THE DAY

That road is *the* big topic. The connection with Tibet and China has been there for some time, while the route south to Kagbeni, Jomsom and on to Pokhara gets more like a road every season. Of course, Himalayan highways can be notoriously fragile constructions: avalanches, floods and other disasters can cut them in seconds and repairs can takes weeks, or longer.

RANDOM FACTS

✪ Throughout the 1960s the CIA supported a low-level guerrilla campaign by fierce Khampa Tibetan warriors based in Mustang, against the Chinese.

✪ The dry climate and infrequent rainfall means buildings can be constructed out of rammed earth or sun-baked mudbricks.

✪ The Ghar Gompa was built to placate demons who had repeatedly destroyed the Samye monastery near Lhasa in Tibet. Once the Ghar Gompa was completed the demons caused no further trouble to the Samye monastery.

MOST BIZARRE SIGHT

Goat herds heading south to the lowland Nepalese markets as winter approaches. Stand aside as they flow by; they can clog the trails.

LOCAL LINGO

A hearty 'Tashi Delek' – hello, greetings, welcome, how are you? – goes a long way in Mustang. It's easy to remember because half the people you meet – male or female – are likely to be named Tashi.

by Ryan Ver Berkmoes

○ **THE YUKON**

NORTH
AMERICA

EUROPE

'This vast and thinly populated wilderness...
has a grandeur and beauty that can only be
appreciated in person'

AUSTRALIA

#4

ACTIVITIES | ADVENTURE | OFF-ROAD

THE YUKON, CANADA

- ○ **POPULATION** 34,000
- ○ **MAIN TOWN** Whitehorse
- ○ **LANGUAGE** English
- ○ **MAJOR INDUSTRIES** Tourism, government, mining
- ○ **UNIT OF CURRENCY** Canadian dollar ($)
- ○ **COST INDEX** Double/dorm room in guesthouse $100/40 (US$100/40), locally brewed Yukon Gold beer $4 (US$4), 16-day kayak rental for the trip to Dawson City $550 (US$550), official campsites $12 (US$12)

WHY GO IN 2013? IT'S NOT GETTING ANY LONELIER OR COLDER

The name Yukon is evocative as well as descriptive: adventure, the far north, wilderness, moose. How can you even hear 'Yukon' and not feel a stirring within? And for good reason. This vast and thinly populated wilderness – most animal species far outnumber humans – has a grandeur and beauty that can only be properly appreciated in person.

But while few places in the world today are so unchanged over the course of time, change has started coming fast to the Yukon. In 2013 it is still one of the least densely populated regions on the planet (there's almost 14.2 sq km/5.5 sq miles for each hardy local) but its tremendous mineral wealth is drawing new residents in a reprise of the fabled Klondike Gold Rush of 1898. Climate change means that parts of the far north are actually dissolving into the Arctic Ocean and the glacier-clad parks are undergoing profound change.

Come and revel in this land – which still puts the wild in wilderness – now.

LIFE-CHANGING EXPERIENCES

Canada's five tallest mountains and the world's largest icefields below the Arctic are all within Kluane National Park. Canoe expeditions down the Yukon River are epic. You'll also appreciate the people; join the funky end-of-the-road vibe of Dawson City, the bustle of Whitehorse and the unique character of villages throughout. The first time you spot a moose wading through a marsh by the side of the road, or a mother

grizzly shepherding her cubs, you'll feel you've really made it to the Yukon.

FESTIVALS & EVENTS

✪ The legendary Yukon Quest, a 1600km dog-sled race, goes from Whitehorse to Fairbanks, Alaska through February darkness and -50°C temperature.

✪ The Yukon River Quest, the world's premier canoe and kayak race, covers the classic 742km run of the Yukon River from Whitehorse to Dawson City in June.

✪ The best tickets for the hugely popular Dawson City Music Festival sell out two months in advance of this late-July party that doubles the town's population.

✪ Discovery Day celebrates gold being found in 1896. On the third Monday in August there are parades and picnics, especially in Dawson City.

WHAT'S HOT...

Betting on early breakup (when the Yukon River thaws for the spring), setting speed records in river kayaks, guys who chop wood all winter for their girlfriends, calling the rest of the world 'outside'

...WHAT'S NOT

Huge projects to run pipelines through the territory, proposals to bring mobile-phone service to places beyond Whitehorse and Dawson, miners who spoil the land, people who want the conveniences of 'outside'

HOT TOPIC OF THE DAY

Mining literally put the Yukon on the map in the late 1890s. News of gold being discovered near today's Dawson City lured thousands of prospectors with dreams of

A DOG SLED TEAM RACING IN
THE YUKON QUEST SLED RACE
BETWEEN FAIRBANKS IN ALASKA
AND WHITEHORSE IN THE YUKON

getting rich quick. Most had no experience and returned home penniless – if they survived at all. The anything-goes gold extraction left disfiguring scars on the landscape that can be seen today. Now the Yukon is in the mist of another boom driven by the record prices of gold and other valuable minerals. But instead of individuals, this time it's huge corporations, and the potential impact on the Yukon is huge. Exploration can scar the land even before extraction and the need for workers is expected to send the population rate soaring by up to double digits. Yukoners have to weigh unexpected new wealth against unexpected new challenges.

RANDOM FACTS

✪ The Yukon is the birthplace of gold-discoverer Keish, aka Skookum Jim

(1855–1916), the Alaska Hwy (1942) and White Fang, the wolf-dog character of the Jack London novel (1906).

✪ Its rich literary tradition includes Robert Service, the poet who immortalised the Yukon through works like *The Shooting of Dan McGrew*.

✪ Aboriginal people continue to hunt and trap as they always have even as they live in villages and drive pickups.

✪ The 68,000 moose outnumber people two to one.

DEFINING FLAVOURS

People eat what they can kill or gather, be it moose or wild berries. But salmon from the Yukon River is a delicacy appreciated the world over. Few Yukon homes won't have racks of the succulent fish smoking during the summer run.

by Carolina Miranda

> 'Go now – while the ruins at Kuélap can be enjoyed in the company of little more than an ethereal layer of cloud-forest mist'

○ **CHACHAPOYAS & KUÉLAP**

#5

ADVENTURE OFF-ROAD CULTURE

CHACHAPOYAS & KUÉLAP, PERU

- ✪ **POPULATION** 24,000
- ✪ **MAIN TOWN** Chachapoyas
- ✪ **LANGUAGES** Spanish, Quechua
- ✪ **MAJOR INDUSTRIES** Agriculture, cattle ranching
- ✪ **UNIT OF CURRENCY** Peruvian Nuevo Sol (S)
- ✪ **COST INDEX** Double room at a B&B S130-160 (US$49-50), admission to ancient ruins at Kuélap S12 (US$4.50), shot of local fruit liqueur S3 (US$1), internet per hour S3 (US$1)

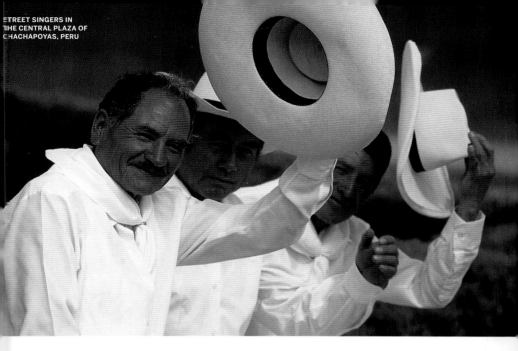

WHY GO IN 2013? A TREASURE TO BE UNCOVERED

Nestled into a minuscule plain in the northern Peruvian Andes, the placid mountain city of Chachapoyas isn't exactly the stuff of traveller lore. For one, it's small, checking in at roughly a dozen blocks around its middle. It's also quiet – the sort of place where the mutts still snooze in the streets and an evening's entertainment consists of strolling around the tidy town centre before sipping a shot of guava liqueur at a combination bar-convenience-liquor store. And it's a pain in the neck to get to – roughly six hours of vertiginous mountain roads from the nearest domestic airport.

But Chachapoyas couldn't be more worthwhile. This charming agricultural centre sits amid some of the country's most incredible cultural and natural treasures. To the south is an entire river valley's worth of pre-Inca ruins, including the majestic citadel of Kuélap, which resides on a mountain-top amid a tangle of cloud forest. To the west is the funerary site of Karajía, a series of adobe sarcophagi tucked into a mountain crevice, all of which are painted to look like human figures, and some of which bear skull headdresses. And to the north is the Catarata de Gocta, one of the world's tallest waterfalls – with a frigid stream that roars over sandstone-coloured rock before plunging into the forested banks of the Cocahuayco River.

For decades, this rugged area has lain largely unexplored by foreign travellers. But that isn't going to last for long. For the past half-dozen years, the Peruvian government has been quietly paving roads and improving other infrastructure to make the area more visitor-friendly. It has also begun to promote the destination as an important historical site. With Machu Picchu deluged by hundreds of thousands of travellers every year, it means that the time to go to Chachapoyas is now – while the nearby ruins at Kuélap can still be enjoyed in the company of little more than an ethereal layer of cloud-forest mist.

LIFE-CHANGING EXPERIENCES

Trips to any of the area's sights will involve going up and down, then down and up one of the area's dizzying Andean roads. (The bumpy access road to Kuélap is a renowned white-knuckler.) But even though the curves can be daunting, the scenery could not be more spectacular: jagged peaks are draped in high-altitude forest and covered in a patchwork of farms. And there's always the possibility of surprise: tucked into various strategic promontories are the remains of long-abandoned Chachapoya villages, some of which are more than a thousand years old.

FESTIVALS & EVENTS

✪ The first week of June, Chachapoyas celebrates Tourism Week with fireworks, horse parades, contests, games, art exhibits and colourful folk dances.
✪ The entire town (down to the Peruvian Paso horses) turns out for special masses and processions in honour of the patron deity, *la Virgen de Asunta* (the Virgin of the Assumption), in the second week of August.

HOT TOPIC OF THE DAY

Chachapoyas has an airport but it's currently used exclusively by the Peruvian Air Force. The site, however, recently received a freshening-up courtesy of a commercial concession, leading to plenty of scuttlebutt that commercial air travel to the area may not be far behind.

MOST BIZARRE SIGHT

With its towering sarcophagi tucked into a visible mountain crevice, Karajía is the area's most iconic burial site. But these are not alone. The Chachapoya planted their dead into mountains all over the Utcubamba River Valley. Pull out a pair of binoculars and you just might find yourself staring at the impassive human likeness of a burial chamber. In Chachapoyas, the dead are always watching.

REGIONAL FLAVOURS

A bit of the Andes and a little of the Amazon is what you'll find on the Chachapoyas table. High altitudes and chilly nights mean that soup is a staple: in particular, *cazuelas*, oversized tubs of clear consommé studded with chicken or beef and potatoes, simmered for hours and flavoured with fresh Andean herbs. Tropical flavours also come in the form of *juanes*, steamy, fist-sized dumplings crafted from seasoned *yuca* (cassava) and meat and then steamed in a *bijao* leaf. Most frequently served at breakfast, these hearty, fragrant treats go down well any time of day.

ANTHROPOMORPHIC WOODEN COFFINS UNDER A CLIFF AT A KARAJÍA FUNERARY SITE, CHACHAPOYAS, PERU

by Carolina Miranda

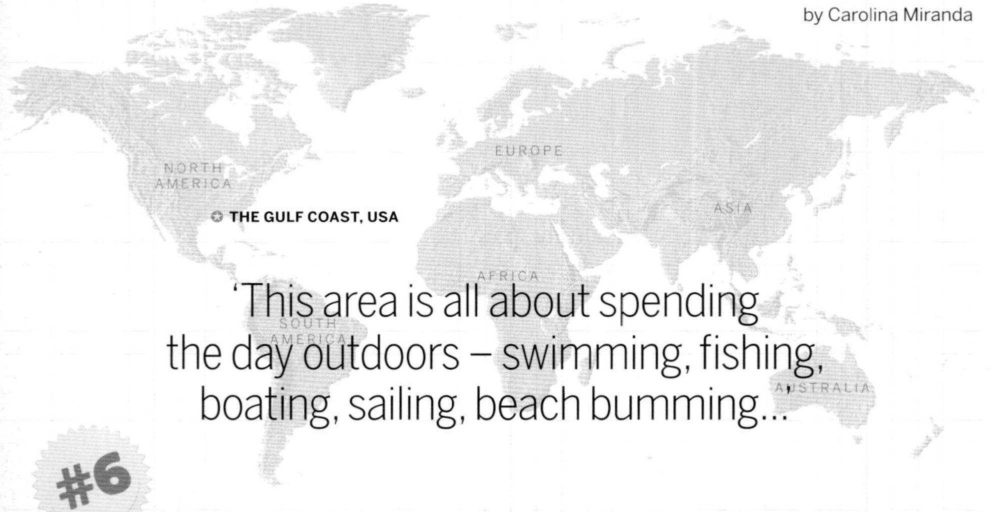

NORTH AMERICA

EUROPE

ASIA

☼ THE GULF COAST, USA

AFRICA

SOUTH AMERICA

AUSTRALIA

'This area is all about spending the day outdoors – swimming, fishing, boating, sailing, beach bumming...

#6

ACTIVITIES VALUE FAMILY

THE GULF COAST, USA

- ☼ **POPULATION** 3.2 million
- ☼ **MAIN TOWNS** New Orleans, Biloxi, Mobile and Pensacola
- ☼ **LANGUAGE** English
- ☼ **MAJOR INDUSTRIES** Petroleum, fishing, military, tourism
- ☼ **UNIT OF CURRENCY** US dollar (US$)
- ☼ **COST INDEX** Shrimp po' boy sandwich US$12, suite for a family of four on the beach in Biloxi US$230-320, admission to the USS *Alabama* battleship US$12, a dozen oysters on the half shell US$8-10

THE MYSTIC KREWE OF
BARKUS PARADE IN NEW
ORLEANS' FRENCH QUARTER

WHY GO IN 2013?
THE COMEBACK COAST

The area of the United States that has become synonymous with the words 'oil spill' doesn't sound like it'd be a vacation must-do. But a lot has happened since a deep-water drilling operation off the coast of Louisiana went fatally awry in 2010. The Gulf Coast – never a place to take disaster lying down – has rebounded. Rolling sand dunes once again sparkle and seasonal travellers are again enjoying the Gulf's tepid waters, not to mention its tender, locally caught fish.

Granted, things aren't perfect. Shrimp harvests are down, some marshes are still mucky and long-term damage has yet to be assessed. But this singular patch of American coast has banded together to make a comeback (with the assistance of $60 million in tourism grants from BP, the oil company that oversaw work on the leaky rig). Effective clean-ups and other post-spill programs can claim part of the credit for the turnaround. But any traveller who's been to the Gulf Coast can tell you that it's hard not to feel loyal to the plucky character of the region, affectionately dubbed 'the Redneck Riviera'.

It's not for nothing that folks have been travelling here for generations. There's Louisiana, with its blazing Mardi Gras parties and its warren of swampy bayous, keepers of singular pockets of French-American culture. There's Mississippi, with its windswept ivory beaches, shoreline

casinos and a billowy new museum designed by Frank Gehry (the Ohr-O'Keefe Museum of Art) in Biloxi. In Alabama, there's a dramatic bay, a battleship from World War II and idyllic patches of seashore. And, in the Florida panhandle, there is all that gleaming crystal-quartz sand that feels like sugar in between the toes. All of this is tied together by roughly 650km of coastline and a zestful appetite for all things seafood, pork sausage and red beans and rice.

Gulf Coast, USA, it's good to have you back.

LIFE-CHANGING EXPERIENCES

This area is all about spending the day outdoors (swimming, fishing, boating, sailing, beach bumming), then coming back to roost at sunset, preferably with an icy drink in hand. And then, of course, there's the cuisine: this is *the* place to dip into fresh trays of silky oysters and some down-home Cajun-Southern cooking. Cheers to that.

FESTIVALS & EVENTS

❂ The Gulf is renowned for its Mardi Gras celebrations and nowhere else are they as rambunctious, licentious or openly drunken as in New Orleans, where you'll find parades, live music, ladies flashing their hoo-hahs and lots of beads. This year, the big party falls on 12 February.

❂ Every year in late April/early May, the planet's biggest names in jazz, R&B and folk descend on New Orleans for the Jazz and Heritage Festival – otherwise known as JazzFest.

RANDOM FACTS

✪ For two decades in the early 18th century, Mobile, Alabama served as the capital of the French territory of Louisiana, before the capital was moved to New Orleans.

✪ During the course of its history, Pensacola has been under the control of five different national governments: the Spanish, the British, the French, the Confederacy and the US. For this reason, it is known as the 'City of the Five Flags'.

MOST BIZARRE SIGHT

Perhaps no event in the US is as delightfully ridiculous as the annual Mullet Toss, held every April at the Florabama, a rickety old honky-tonk that sits on the beach at the Alabama–Florida state line. The goal: to imbibe vast quantities of beer, devour lots of crawfish and then toss a dead mullet fish into Alabama from the Florida side of the border. Truly sublime.

REGIONAL FLAVOURS

Welcome to Cajun country! This part of the United States is renowned for its cooking – a savoury melange of spicy sausage, buttery sauces and piquant bisques, as well as countless other permutations of French Creole traditions. The Louisiana area is the beating heart of Cajun cuisine, but you'll find its influences all over the Gulf – namely in the form of stewed red beans, spicy gumbos bursting with pork and seafood, and heaping po' boy sandwiches: two slabs of baguette stuffed full of fresh fried shrimp, crawfish or oysters. It's hard to make a belly any happier than this.

by Joe Bindloss

EUROPE
○ **CARINTHIA, AUSTRIA**

NORTH
AMERICA

ASIA

'...Carinthia dilutes the Austrian efficiency with Mediterranean laissez-faire'

AUSTRALIA

#7

ACTIVITIES | VALUE | FAMILY

CARINTHIA, AUSTRIA

- ○ **POPULATION** 560,600
- ○ **MAIN TOWN** Klagenfurt
- ○ **LANGUAGES** German, Slovene
- ○ **MAJOR INDUSTRIES** Tourism, engineering, forestry
- ○ **UNIT OF CURRENCY** Euro (€)
- ○ **COST INDEX** Glass of beer €3.30 (US$4.30), two-course meal €20-30 (US$26-39), hotel double/dorm room for a night €100/25 (US$130/33), ski pass per day/week €40/220 (US$52/288), internet access per hour €4 (US$5.20)

SUMMER PURSUITS ON LAKE OSSIACH IN CARINTHIA, AUSTRIA

WHY GO IN 2013? IT'S THE ALPS YOU CAN STILL AFFORD!

With belts tightening across Europe, the Alps are fast becoming the exclusive preserve of the champagne set...again. Lesser mortals are having to think twice before booking that ski trip to Trois Vallées or a summer weekend on Lake Geneva. That's where Carinthia (Kärnten) comes into its own. Long overlooked in favour of more showy corners of the Alps, Austria's southernmost province offers all the rugged scenery and winter powder, without the Swiss banker price tag.

With ski resorts nestled on every mountaintop, Carinthia is best known outside Austria for uncrowded slopes and après-ski where you don't have to take out a second mortgage just to buy a beer.

Locals would rather you didn't find out about Carinthia in summer; from June to August, families gambol in geothermally heated lakes that simmer at almost bathtub temperatures, and stroll in broad valleys that trap the sun for longer than anywhere else in Austria.

Why more people don't know about this peaceful corner of the Alps is a mystery. Backing onto Italy and Slovenia, Carinthia dilutes the Austrian efficiency with Mediterranean laissez-faire. Add a shake of stunning scenery, a squirt of quirky cuisine and a handful of eccentric festivals, and you should have a recipe for Alpine perfection. So where are the crowds? Check out Carinthia now, while peace and quiet reigns, because it won't stay like this forever.

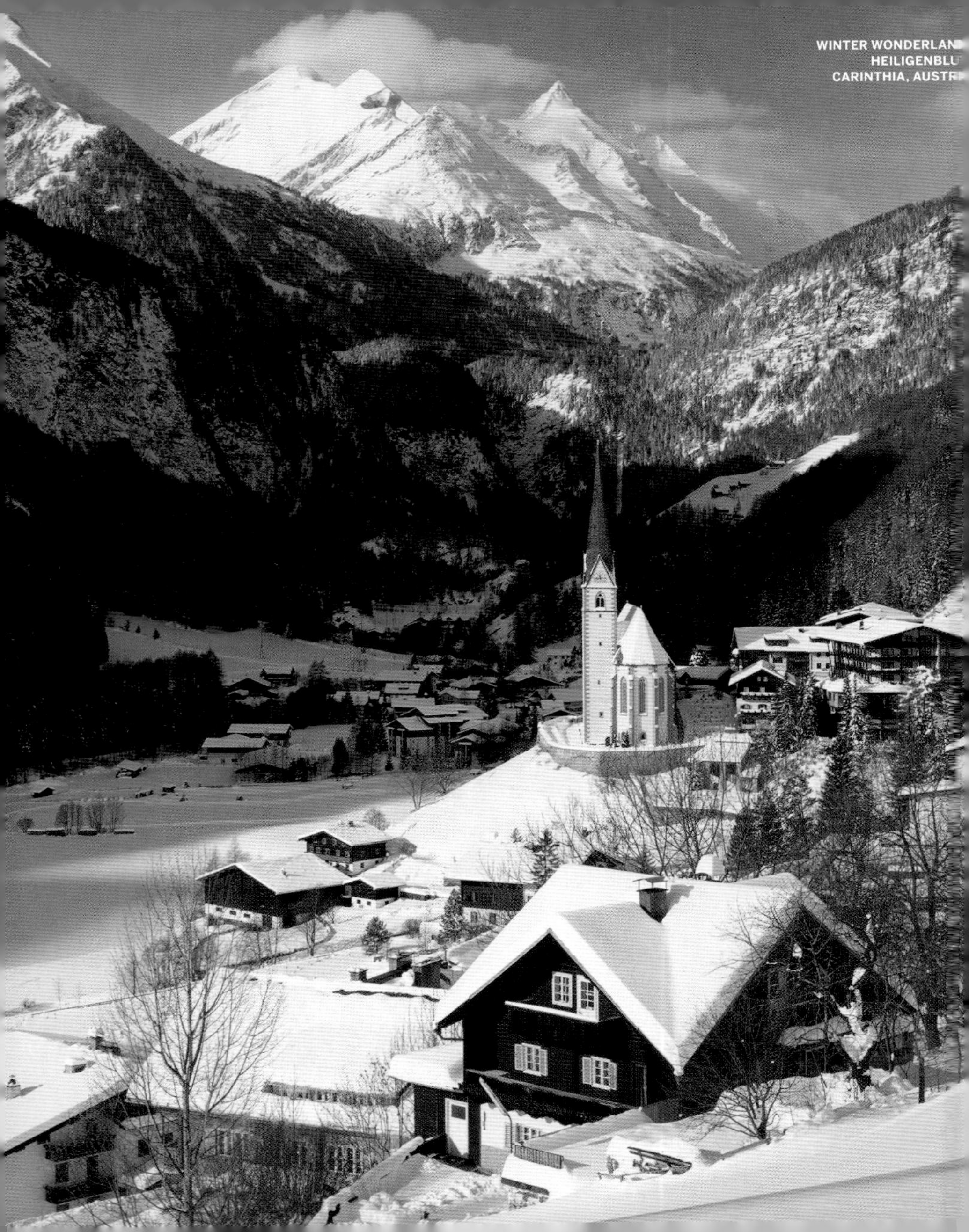

WINTER WONDERLAN
HEILIGENBLU
CARINTHIA, AUSTR

LIFE-CHANGING EXPERIENCES

Water is the attraction in this laid-back corner of the Alps. In summer, the languorous lakes of Wörthersee, Faakersee, Ossiachersee and Millstättersee earn Carinthia its Austrian Riviera nickname. With natural central-heating from geothermal springs, water temperature can reach 26°C, on par with the Mediterranean, perfect for swimming, paddling or floating dinners for two on a raft (a popular diversion on Millstättersee). Think of it as a less-exclusive, family-friendly alternative to the Italian lakes, with fewer villas but more apple strudel.

FESTIVALS & EVENTS

✪ On the first Sunday in February, locals gather in front of the town dairy in Stein to be pelted with bread rolls as part of a 1000-year-old festival to celebrate the generosity of local noblewoman Hildegard von Stein.

✪ Church opera (exactly what it says on the tin) is the hallmark of the Carinthia Summer Music Festival, with music events at churches, stately homes and castles across the province from July to August.

✪ Normally tranquil Faakersee gets a wake-up call every September from 70,000 throbbing motorcycle engines for European Bike Week; think leather, Harleys, heavy rock, facial hair.

RECENT FAD

An icier version of riding a river on an old inner tube, snowtubing is all the rage in Carinthia. The resort of Nassfeld is the focal point for the family-friendly fun, with dedicated runs where you can launch yourself downhill on a giant inflatable doughnut.

HOT TOPIC OF THE DAY

The topic people would prefer you *didn't* mention is Jörg Haider, the former governor of Carinthia, still ruffling feathers years after his death. The furore over Haider's stance on immigration has died down; these days, the conversational no-go areas are his role in the collapse of Hypo Alpe-Adria Bank, and the court case that made it illegal to suggest that Haider had a secret gay lifestyle.

MOST BIZARRE SIGHT

Most people will be surprised to learn that the world's most famous sports car has its origins in an old sawmill in the mountain town of Gmünd in western Carinthia. After WWII, Ferry Porsche retreated here to create a car that was worthy of his love of driving – and lo, the Porsche 356 was born. The birth of the Porsche marque is celebrated at the Helmut Pfeifhofer Porsche Museum, a shrine to speed with more than 40 vintage Porsches, including the Porsche 911 driven by local traffic cops (presumably to keep up with other Porsche drivers).

REGIONAL FLAVOURS

Noodles are Carinthia's unlikely contribution to the European cooking canon. It's a little-known fact that the word noodle came to the English language from the German *nudeln,* used to describe a whole family of pasta-like treats from the Eastern Alps. In Carinthia, *nudeln* most commonly take the form of pasta pouches, stuffed with curd cheese, potato or minced meat. On special occasions, look out for *kletzennudeln,* pudding pasta stuffed with a tantalising mix of dried pears, cinnamon, honey and nuts.

by Rafael Wlodarski

'...travellers willing to make the trek out to the Philippines' western fringes can expect adventure to be served up by the spoonful'

PALAWAN, THE PHILIPPINES ○

#8

PALAWAN, THE PHILIPPINES

ADVENTURE | OFF-ROAD | BEACH

- ○ **POPULATION** 2.6 million
- ○ **MAIN TOWN** Puerto Princesa
- ○ **LANGUAGE** Tagalog (Filipino)
- ○ **MAJOR INDUSTRY** Agriculture
- ○ **UNIT OF CURRENCY** Philippine Peso (P)
- ○ **COST INDEX** Cup of coffee P40 (US$.95), internet access per hour P20 (US$0.50), pension/double hotel room P900/2100 (US$21/50), short tricycle ride P30 (US$0.70)

WHY GO IN 2013? ADVENTURES IN THE ECOLOGICAL FRONTIER

Although its rowdy Philippine neighbour Boracay may be the darling of the beach-hopping jetset – *Travel & Leisure* voted it the fourth-best island destination in the world – sedate Palawan manages to impress without need of such baubles. Stretching between Mindoro Strait and Borneo, Palawan incorporates thousands of sparkling, rugged islands and is fringed by 2000km of pristine coastline. Sparsely populated and with nary a traveller to be seen, that's a lot of beach real estate to go around. So far Palawan's natural marvels have only been sampled by plucky backpackers willing to brave the region's dusty roads and walloping distances in search of adventure. Not for much longer. The trail these pioneers have blazed is set to explode, with regional airlines waking up to Palawan's potential and clambering to schedule direct flights to the capital. Throw in the mushrooming growth of style-conscious boutique hotels normally found in places like Ko Samui or Bali, and you can feel that Palawan is ready to hit the big-time in 2013.

Chiselled out of the Sulu Sea and isolated from the hubbub of other Philippine islands, Palawan today remains one of the country's last ecological frontiers. The hardy island interiors heave with mountain ranges carpeted by thick jungle, while at water's edge the virgin shoreline melts into a mantle of coral swarming with marine life. Throw in some underground rivers, towering limestone karsts, world-class diving, shipwrecks and infinite island-hopping opportunities, and you have the proverbial Garden of Eden on your hands. Although sporadic public transport and the lack of paved roads mean that these isles do not lend themselves to easy exploration, travellers willing to make the trek out to the Philippines' western fringes can expect adventure to be served up by the spoonful.

LIFE-CHANGING EXPERIENCES

✪ Exploring the jaw-dropping underground rivers of St Paul Subterranean National Park is unforgettable. Navigable by boat, the 8km-long river system weaves deep under limestone cliffs and through gaping caves before spilling its turquoise waters into the Sulu Sea.

✪ Jungle trekking through untouched rainforest interiors will have you coming face-to-face with troops of monkeys, giant monitor lizards and a rainbow swath of birdlife.

✪ Visitors should not leave without island-hopping around the Calamian Islands – with hundreds of picture-perfect beaches and coves, volcano-heated lagoons, snorkelling reefs, and world-class diving among fish-packed WWII Japanese wrecks.

FESTIVALS & EVENTS

✪ The Easter Holy Week sees sombre re-enactments of Christ's last days, sometimes with enough gory enthusiasm to make Mel Gibson proud.

✪ The ancient springtime Lambay festival celebrates the beginning of the traditional hunting-and-gathering season, with Batak tribesmen thrusting about hunting tools during re-enactments of the hunt.

✪ Celebrated by the Tagbuana people in April, the Pagdiwata Ritual Festival involves the giving of thanks to traditional deities and asking for help in the healing of the sick.

✪ In May, the Pasinggatan Festival is yet another opportunity to release the unbridled Filipino passion for music and dance.

RANDOM FACTS

✪ Palawan is comprised of 1780 islands and boasts 1959km of coastline!

✪ Three major indigenous communities are found in Palawan: Batak in the central and northern regions, Pala'wan in the south, and Tagbanua throughout.

MOST BIZARRE SIGHT

In 2009 a massive species of carnivorous pitcher plant large enough to devour creatures the size of rats was discovered in the Palawan highlands.

REGIONAL FLAVOURS

Although much of its regional cuisine is based on dishes from the Visayas and Mindanao, Palawan dishes are famous for using green mango to provide a sour kick to many meals. Not surprisingly, seafood features dominantly, though one local delicacy stands out: *tamilok*. Although it's called a woodworm, this mollusc is actually a type of unusual saltwater clam that bores into submerged wood – particularly rotting mangrove roots. Thin, long and slippery, *tamilok* is served raw, eaten by hand and swallowed whole like a slimy, foot-long oyster. In a tradition of belated Dutch courage, it is often followed by a swift swig of local hard liquor.

TAGBANUA TRIBESMAN
PADDLING ON LAKE KAYANGAN
ON CORON ISLAND, PART OF THE
CALAMIAN ISLANDS, PALAWAN

by Laura Crawford

NORTH AMERICA

EUROPE

ASIA

○ **INLAND SEA, JAPAN**

AUSTRALIA

'Many of the islands...offer the chance to experience Japan without all the bells, whistles and bullet trains'

#9

ACTIVITIES | **OFF-ROAD** | **CULTURE**

INLAND SEA, JAPAN

- ○ **POPULATION** 35 million
- ○ **MAIN TOWNS** Hiroshima, Takamatsu, Onomichi, Matsuyama, Iwakuni
- ○ **LANGUAGE** Japanese
- ○ **MAJOR INDUSTRIES** Fishing, ship building, agriculture, tourism
- ○ **UNIT OF CURRENCY** Yen (¥)
- ○ **COST INDEX** Glass of beer ¥600 (US$7), plate of grilled oysters ¥1300 (US$15), night in a *minshuku* (family-run lodgings) per person with meals ¥5000-9000 (US$60-108), bicycle hire per day ¥500 (US$6)

WHY GO IN 2013? FINE ARTS AWAY FROM IT ALL

Tokyo, Kyoto, Mt Fuji...the islands of the Seto Inland Sea? You'd be forgiven if the name of this stretch of water in Japan's west doesn't ring any bells. With the exception of Miyajima and its oft-photographed vermillion 'floating' *torii* (shrine gate), most of the Inland Sea islands aren't on the usual tourist hit list. Fair enough. They're out of the way and there's just so much to *do* in Tokyo.

But those who make the effort are rewarded. Many of the islands in this roughly 400km-long waterway offer the chance to experience Japan without all the bells, whistles and bullet trains. Catch a sea breeze while strolling down a narrow village lane, hike to a hillside temple, stay in a traditional inn, or just sit back and sigh at the blue-green water vistas. On some islands, see how the new is finding its place alongside the traditional. Take arty isle Naoshima, where you can explore world-class contemporary art museums before retiring to your *minshuku* (guesthouse).

And what better time to drop by than 2013, when the second Setouchi Triennale Art Festival rolls around, this time held over three separate seasons with art, music and drama events and exhibitions on some 11 islands. Let the island-hopping begin.

LIFE-CHANGING EXPERIENCES

For the rare thrill of cycling 50m above the sea, ride the *Shimanami Kaidō* (Shimanami Sea Route), a highway with a monster chain

STONE LANTERN AND ITSUKUSHIMA
JINJA SHRINE, MIYAJIMA ISLAND,
HIROSHIMA, JAPAN

of suspension bridges linking Japan's main island Honshū with Shikoku, via six small islands. If you prefer less pedalling, try sleeping in a Mongolian tent on Naoshima, soaking in a sea-view *rotenburo* (outdoor bath) on Manabe-shima, or walking in the 1200-year-old footsteps of revered monk Kūkai (aka Kōbo Daishi) at Mt Misen on the holy island of Itsukushima.

FESTIVALS & EVENTS

☼ The Setouchi Triennale Art Festival runs 20 March to 21 April, 20 July to 1 September and 5 October to 4 November.

☼ *Nōren Kabuki* (rural *kabuki*, stylised traditional theatre) has been performed on the island of Shōdo-shima for about 300 years. Two thatch-roofed outdoor stages remain, where you can see performances in early May and mid-October.

☼ In late July Miyajima's Kangen Festival, a Shintō ritual, sees decorated wooden boats float by under the night sky to the sound of traditional drums and flutes.

☼ O-bon, when ancestral spirits are honoured throughout Japan, is especially stirring on the island of Shiraishi, where in mid-August the traditional *bon-odori* (bon-festival dance) is performed on the beach as it has been for centuries, and lanterns are sent bobbing out to sea.

HOT TOPIC OF THE DAY

As the young are predictably lured away by big-city opportunities, depopulation on the islands is a serious issue. There is much talk of revitalisation, with art sites, galleries and artist-in-residence programs among the initiatives to attract new stayers and draw in the tourists.

RANDOM FACTS

☼ An abundance of passing ships and all the handy hidden coves once made the Inland Sea prime territory for pirates.

☼ Stone from quarries on Shōdo-shima was used in the early 1600s to reconstruct Osaka Castle.

☼ Setonaikai National Park covers swathes of the Inland Sea and is one of Japan's oldest national parks (designated in 1934).

MOST BIZARRE SIGHT

What does a steel-tube magnate and arms manufacturer do when his beloved mother dies? Become a Buddhist priest and put his fortune into building an elaborate temple complex, of course. Kōsan-ji, on Ikuchi-jima, is the garish result of one man's love for his mother and includes, among its many features, decorative gates, a pagoda, and a cave of 1000 Buddhas where you can view several illustrations of hell.

REGIONAL FLAVOURS

No surprises here – seafood is the star across the region, so you're in for a treat if you love nothing more than a plate of fresh sushi. *Kaki* (oysters) are a raw, grilled or crumbed-and-fried speciality on Miyajima, and *tako* (octopus) is the central character in *suigun-nabe*, a seafood-laden hotpot on Ikuchi-jima. Head to Onomichi for a hearty bowl of *rāmen* (thin noodles in broth) with pork, or to Takamatsu for *sanuki udon* (thick white noodles). Elsewhere, the mild climate means citrus groves flourish – try the local *mikan* (mandarins). For something a tad unexpected, how about olives? Shōdo-shima is famous for them.

by Abigail Blasi

EUROPE

NORTH AMERICA

○ **CAMPANIA, ITALY**

ASIA

AFRICA

SOUTH

AUSTRALIA

'....even its harshest critics can't deny the complex allure of its volcanic geography, beautiful coastline, mad energy, and punchy cuisine'

10

CULTURE   FOOD   FAMILY

CAMPANIA, ITALY

- ○ **POPULATION** 5.8 million
- ○ **MAIN TOWN** Naples
- ○ **LANGUAGES** Italian, Neapolitan
- ○ **MAJOR INDUSTRIES** Construction, textiles, food processing, metallurgy
- ○ **UNIT OF CURRENCY** Euro (€)
- ○ **COST INDEX** Cappuccino €1 (US$1.30), hotel double/dorm room for a night from €60/18 (US$79/24), short taxi ride €5 (US$6.60), slice of pizza €2 (US$2.60)

WHY GO IN 2013? CHARISMATIC CAMPANIA'S CULTURAL INJECTION

Campania, a region of Italy with a permanent twinkle in its eye, is already home to Italy's most sumptuous stretch of coastline (the Amalfi Coast), one of the 'beautiful country's' most mind-blowing and ebullient cities (Naples), the menacing beauty of Mt Vesuvius and the frozen-in-lava ancient Roman city of Pompeii. This epic region is where Icarus fell, Odysseus outwitted the sirens and Aeneus took a trip to Hades.

But this year Campania has even more reason to have a swagger in its step, as it's receiving an enormous injection of cash, with €500 million flowing into the west Naples district alone. It's all part of its role in hosting the UN's fourth Universal Forum of Cultures from April to July.

Events will include art exhibitions from all five continents, music, cinema, dance, street artists and theatre, circus acts, food markets and workshops.

LIFE-CHANGING EXPERIENCES

✪ Make your way along the epic Amalfi Coast, a scenic rollercoaster, where soaring cliffs meet azure seas, the hills are dotted with fragrant lemon groves, and pastel-hued medieval villages cling to the vine-covered slopes.

✪ Visit the ghostly remains of Pompeii, the busy Roman city that was forever frozen in time when Mt Vesuvius erupted on 24 August AD 79. You'll see the extraordinarily preserved ruins of what was a busy commercial centre, and some awe-inspiring ancient Roman frescoes.

FESTIVALS & EVENTS

✪ From 11 to 19 May, Bagnoli, a western suburb of Naples, will host the America's Cup World Series, bringing the cream of the world's sailors to Italy to race in futuristic AC45 wing-sailed catamarans.

✪ In June, it's the turn of Amalfi to host the Palio delle Quattro Antiche Repubbliche Marinare. This annual traditional regatta shifts locations among the four ancient maritime republics – the others being Venice, Genoa and Pisa. The boating competition is preceded by a grand medieval parade complete with flag bearers, horses, drummers and trumpet players.

RECENT FAD

After years of rubbish-collection crises, thought to have been exacerbated by the *Camorra* (local mafia), some closure has been brought...by regularly shipping the region's rubbish to the Netherlands.

HOT TOPIC OF THE DAY

The 2013 election: the first since Berlusconi was replaced by the 'technocrats'. Will influential comedian Beppe Grillo make it into office?

DEFINING DIFFERENCE

Campania is famous for its sense of humour and sense of anarchy. There's something intangibly extreme here; for example, at New Year, when Italians set off fireworks to celebrate, there are usually more accidents in Campania than anywhere else in Italy. The region is a furiously creative place, famous for its theatre and comedians. Before Italian unification in 1860, Naples was one of Europe's most

brilliantly cultured cities. Many Italian traditions were born here: it was the first place to top pizza with tomatoes, and to host a comic opera. Goethe, who visited in the 19th century, said, 'Naples is a paradise: Everyone lives in a state of intoxicated self-forgetfulness.' Today Campania attracts a contradictory cocktail of accolades and infuriated critiques, but even its harshest critics can't deny the complex allure of its volcanic geography, beautiful coastline, mad energy and punchy cuisine.

LOCAL LINGO

Neapolitan is spoken in Naples and the surrounding area of Campania, and

rather than being a variant on Italian, is a language all of its own, officially recognised as such by the region in 2008, and remains very much the language of the people. It's unintelligible to those who speak only Italian, with its own grammar, pronunciation and vocabulary. It evolved from the Latin spoken by Roman invaders, and was afterwards influenced by different settlers in and invaders of the area: the Greeks, Normans, French and Spanish.

- *yamme* (let's go; Italian: *andiamo*)
- *va buo* (OK; Italian: *va bene*)
- *munno* (world; Italian: *mondo*)
- *guaglione/a* = boy/girl; Italian: *giovanotto/a*)

REGIONAL FLAVOURS

Campania is world renowned for its delicious *pizza Napolitana*, which has a thicker crust than the paper-thin incarnations further north. The region's exuberance is reflected by what it serves on the table. Vegetables and herbs grown in the fertile soil around Mt Vesuvius form the base for many flavourful dishes, which often include capers, pasta and fresh buffalo mozzarella. Fresh-from-the-sea fish and shellfish also feature, while the area is also famous for its richly exotic pastries, in which the use of honey, nuts and spices displays unmistakeable Arab and Greek influences.

by Rafael Wlodarski

'…San Francisco continues to attract kindred spirits, eagerly embracing all newcomers to the bosom of its cultural mélange'

#1

EVENTS CULTURE FOOD

SAN FRANCISCO, USA

- **POPULATION** 805,235
- **FOREIGN VISITORS PER YEAR** 4.7 million
- **LANGUAGE** English
- **UNIT OF CURRENCY** US dollar ($)
- **COST INDEX** Cup of coffee US$2.50, cable-car ride US$5, dorm room/double hotel room US$25/120

WHY GO IN 2013?
THE AMERICA'S CUP!

As gorgeous as it is eccentric, San Francisco is the darling of America's west coast. Famous for hills, earthquakes and a penchant for liberal politics, this is the city that introduced the world to denim jeans, inspired the beat generation to go on the road, gave the first hippies a place to sit-in and thrust gay rights into the collective conscience. Today San Francisco continues to attract kindred spirits, eagerly embracing all newcomers to the bosom of its cultural mélange. In no other town are you as likely to see scions of Silicon Valley propping up the same bar as skinny-jeaned culture vultures, Meso-American immigrants and brassy drag-queen divas.

The city's fine edifice has aged gracefully over the years – a whiff of bygone charm clings to its jaunty Victorian abodes, rattling cable cars and that gloriously Art Deco bridge. Add to this some of the best dining options in the world, an explosive street-art scene, dozens of raucous festivals and a photogenic backdrop of foggy San Francisco Bay, and you can imagine how hard it is to leave before you even get here.

In the unlikely event that you need an extra incentive to get yourself to San Francisco, the city has an ace up its sleeve – the 34th America's Cup is coming to fog city in 2013. Big changes and upgrades are afoot all along San Francisco's heaving waterfront, with smart new businesses setting up shop to take advantage of sensational Bay Area views.

LIFE-CHANGING EXPERIENCES

✪ The iconic Golden Gate Bridge is a marvel of cable-suspension engineering – bike over its span and hike up the Marin Headlands for postcard-perfect vistas.

✪ Alcatraz Island, home to America's most infamous prison, rather ironically sports some of the best views of both the city and the Golden Gate Bridge.

✪ Born in San Francisco, the California Cuisine creed embraces fresh local produce and inventive fusion. The city's enviable eating options can satisfy any palate.

FESTIVALS & EVENTS

✪ The Valentine's Day Pillow Fight, begun as a flash-mob gathering, has become a firm calendar fixture. Thousands of strangers descend on downtown to whack each other with pillows. We kid you not, this is the most fun you can have with your pyjamas on.

✪ The most gay-friendly city in the world throws one of the most impressive LGBTQ festivals around. SF Pride (June) heaves with tourists, sequins, wigs, flesh, boas, hugs, music and revelry into the night.

✪ Catering to 'specialist' sexual proclivities, the Folsom Street Fair (September) is dedicated to bondage, S&M and anything leather. Get ready to see more arse-less chaps than you can poke a riding crop at.

✪ Dia de los Muertos (Day of the Dead), a traditional Central American festival, is observed on All Saints Day (1 November) and includes a candlelit procession, music and art honouring the dead.

RECENT FAD

Independent food carts and trucks are all the rage. Live-tweeting their locations to hungry digerati, mobile-food collectives serve up everything from Korean tacos to crème-brulée-to-go to Jamaican jerk chicken.

WHAT'S HOT...

Parklets: guerrilla art installations commandeering metered-parking spots to create temporary microparks

...WHAT'S NOT

Chain-store coffee: no competition for fresh-roasted artisanal coffee and fine barista-ship

RANDOM FACTS

✪ The first America's Cup race rounded the Isle of Wight in the UK in 1851. It was won by a schooner called *America* – hence the name of the trophy.

✪ San Francisco boasts more restaurants and patents per capita than any other city.

CLASSIC RESTAURANT EXPERIENCE

For all its high-end eateries, nothing beats wandering into a hole-in-the wall *taqueria*, grabbing a wobbly plastic table and attempting to finish the pinnacle of Tex-Mex gastronomy, executed to greasy perfection: the burrito. Everybody you meet will *swear* by a different *taqueria*: to find the 'best', ask seven locals and take the average.

BEST SHOPPING

Valencia St corridor, in painfully hip Mission district, is a microcosm of San-Fran culture. Expect to find independent retailers hocking '50s vintage gear, life-size movie props, vinyl records, authentic pirate supplies, vegan shoes, contemporary art, dog-eared books, modernist furniture and so much more.

by Karla Zimmerman

NORTH AMERICA

☉ **AMSTERDAM**

EUROPE

ASIA

AUSTRALIA

'...the party ramps up in 2013, when more anniversaries than you can shake a herring at coincide'

#2

EVENTS   CULTURE   FOOD

AMSTERDAM, THE NETHERLANDS

- ✪ **POPULATION** 780,600
- ✪ **FOREIGN VISITORS PER YEAR** 4 million
- ✪ **LANGUAGES** Dutch, English
- ✪ **UNIT OF CURRENCY** Euro (€)
- ✪ **COST INDEX** Glass of beer €3 (US$3.90), hotel double €110-160 (US$144-209), *frites* with mayo €3 (US$3.90), bike rental per day €13 (US$17)

WHY GO IN 2013? LOTS OF BIRTHDAY CAKE

Amsterdam's Golden Age charm and progressive attitude always cast a spell on travellers, but the party ramps up big-time in 2013, when more anniversaries than you can shake a herring at coincide. The famed canal ring turns 400 years old. It's Vincent van Gogh's 160th birthday and the 40th for his colour-swirled museum. The Rijksmuseum re-opens after a 10-year renovation, splashing Rembrandts, Vermeers and 7500 other masterpieces over 1.5km of galleries. The Royal Concertgebouw Orchestra – often considered the world's best (and not just because they played on *The Big Lebowski* soundtrack) – blows out 125 candles. Plus the Artis Royal Zoo and Felix Meritis cultural centre mark 175 years and 225 years, respectively. It all adds up to a slew of celebratory concerts, exhibits and street fests grooving throughout 2013.

LIFE-CHANGING EXPERIENCES

Pull up a stool and hoist a beer in a candlelit 'brown' cafe. Most have been in business for 300 years or so, and earn their name from the smoke-stained walls. A wander through the Red Light District will make your jaw go limp, even if near-naked women beckoning from backlit windows is the oldest Amsterdam cliché. At the other end

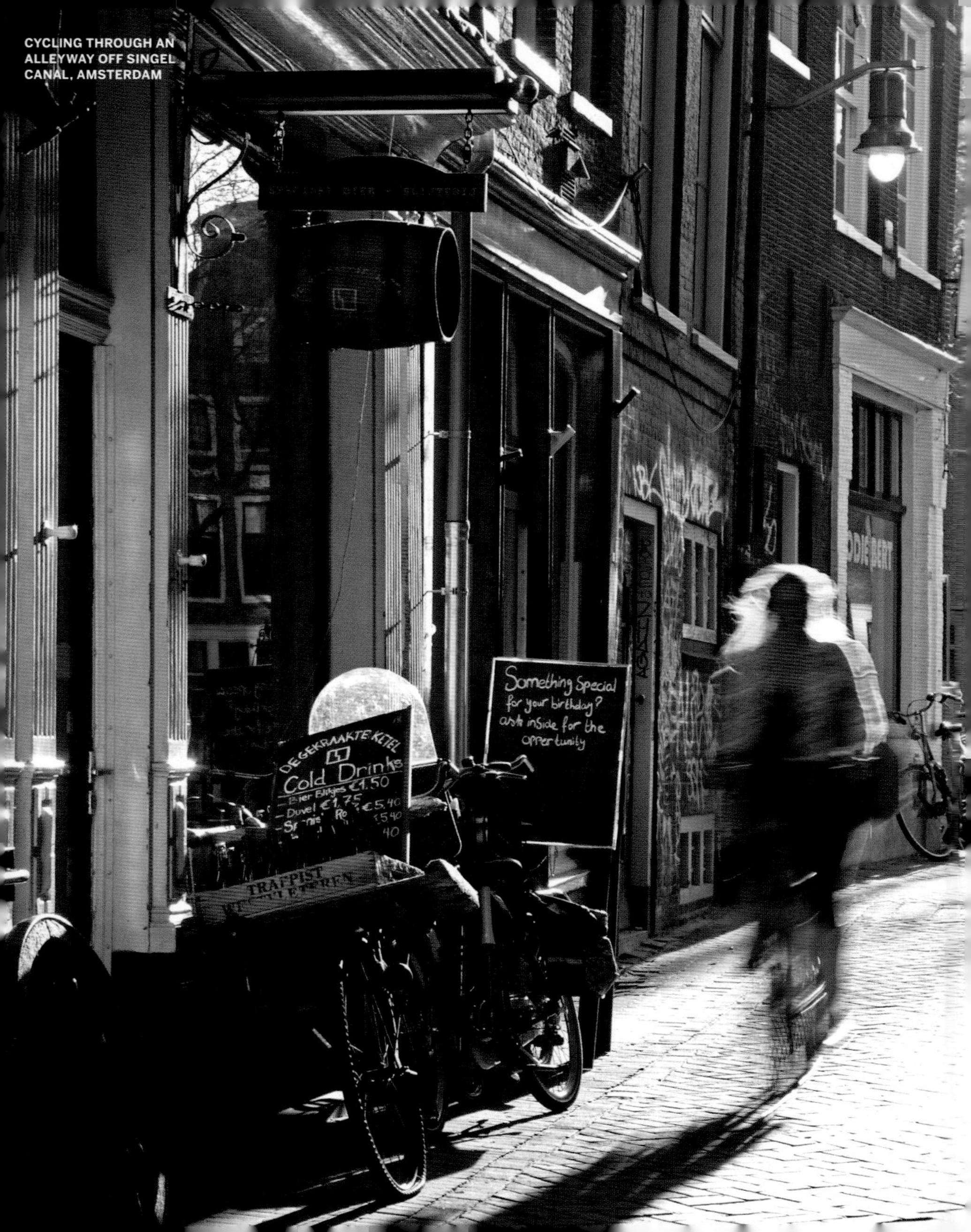

CYCLING THROUGH AN ALLEYWAY OFF SINGEL CANAL, AMSTERDAM

of the spectrum, Anne Frank's melancholy bedroom and diary, sitting in its glass case, provides a heartbreaking WWII flashback.

FESTIVALS & EVENTS

✪ Queen's Day (Koninginnedag) celebrates the monarch's birthday every 30 April. Uproarious boozing, throbbing techno music and the entire population dressed in ridiculous orange outfits set the scene for the rip-roaring street party.

✪ In August the Grachtenfestival (Canal Festival) floats classical concerts around the city's waterways – many performances literally take place on boats. Expect extra action for the canal ring's 400th anniversary.

✪ The International Documentary Film Festival Amsterdam rocks 25 years of screen time come November. Yes, it's another big 2013 birthday, and the festival will honour it with films about Amsterdam made by Amsterdammers.

RANDOM FACTS

✪ More bicycles than people fill the city: there are 881,000 two-wheelers versus about 781,000 citizens. Fifty-eight percent of locals cycle daily.

✪ Arriving at Amsterdam's airport, your plane lands 4.5m below sea level. The city would be underwater were it not built on huge stakes driven into the ground. Centraal Station has 6000 of them keeping it afloat.

✪ Amsterdam has more canals than Venice, with 1281 bridges arching over the water.

HOT TOPIC OF THE DAY

A weed pass, man. In January 2013, new laws will ban foreigners from toking in the city's coffeeshops. Only Dutch residents who have a one-year pass will be able to purchase pot. Politicians initiated the legislation, citing gang-related crime and health risks, but Amsterdammers fought it, saying the new law would drive the trade underground. As of press time, it was still a wait-and-see issue. But it's possible by the time you're reading this, only card-carrying Dutch residents will be able to light up.

CLASSIC RESTAURANT EXPERIENCE

Open since the 1940s, Van Dobben's specialises in traditional Dutch fare: try the *pekelvlees* (something close to corned beef), or make it a *halfom* – *pekelvlees* mixed with liver. In winter, supplement with a bowl of *erwtensoep*, a thick pea soup with smoked sausage and bacon. Van Dobben's *kroketten* (croquettes) rule the town and are compulsory after a late-night booze-up.

BEST SHOPPING

The Negen Straatjes (Nine Little Streets) comprise a tic-tac-toe board of tiny shops dealing in antiques, vintage fashions, housewares and oddball specialities ranging from toothbrushes to velvet ribbons to doll repairs. Atmospheric pubs, cafes and wine bars pop up in their midst, making it easy to wander away the day here.

MOST UNUSUAL PLACE TO STAY

Xaviera's Happy House is a one of a kind, just like owner Xaviera Hollander. The former madam and author of *The Happy Hooker* welcomes guests to her B&B in the ritzy Beethovenstraat neighbourhood. Rooms are decked out with erotic photos, red heart pillows, and books, such as her most recent *Guide to Mind-Blowing Sex*.

by Amy Karafin

NORTH
AMERICA

EUROPE

ASIA

○ **HYDERABAD**

AFRICA

'Elegant and blossoming, but also weathered and undiscovered, the Old City is ripe for exploration'

#3

$ VALUE

CULTURE

FOOD

HYDERABAD, INDIA

- ○ **POPULATION** 7.7 million
- ○ **FOREIGN VISITORS PER YEAR** 322,825
- ○ **LANGUAGES** Telugu, Urdu
- ○ **UNIT OF CURRENCY** Rupee (₹)
- ○ **COST INDEX** Plate of biryani ₹100-200 (US$2-4), double room in a minor heritage building/major palace ₹1650/19,500 (US$30/380), short autorickshaw ride ₹20 (US$0.40), admission to royal sites ₹10-150 (US$0.20-2)

THE TOMB OF THE QUTB SHAHI DYNASTY IS ONE OF HYDERABAD'S HIGHLIGHTS

WHY GO 2013? THE ROYAL SECRETS ARE OUT

Hyderabad was once the capital of a filthy-rich princely state, with the world's largest collection of gems and the world's richest man. The last nizam wore the same thing every day, was said to spend his days smoking opium and composing poetry in Persian, and used a US$90 million, 185-carat diamond, which he found in one of his father's slippers, as a paperweight. He had cars pin-striped in ivory, 38 servants (out of 11,000) employed only to polish chandeliers, 42 concubines and 15 million subjects. Local gem mines kept the money flowing, which generations of

nizams used to build fanciful structures and pleasure gardens across the city.

After India's independence, the palaces and pleasure gardens were sold off, built over and looted, and you had to be really sharp to see the city's beauty. But several palaces in Hyderabad's Old City have recently been refurbished, including Falaknuma Palace, a seven-star hotel (yes, there is such a thing) that was skilfully restored by the Taj Group and is now an exceedingly plush time capsule. Other monuments and buildings are being fixed up, but the city, and many of its architectural gems, are still off the radar and require a little hunting – which keeps

DOWNTOWN HYDERABAD

the masses at bay. Elegant and blossoming, but also weathered and undiscovered, Hyderabad's Old City is ripe for exploration.

LIFE-CHANGING EXPERIENCES

Falaknuma is where you can most easily imagine yourself as royalty, but the Purani Haveli (now HEH the Nizam's Museum) and Chowmahalla palaces are also conducive to regal fantasies. Chowmahalla has a durbar hall with gargantuan Belgian chandeliers, period rooms full of bling and *tchotchkes*, and displays of outrageously ornate clothing, palanquins, swords and cars. It also has the Royal Photo Studio, where you can dress up like a princess and get your sepia-tone picture taken. Displays of the seventh nizam's lush architectural

tastes are all over town, as are lunches of superb Hyderabadi biryani – a rice dish with Persian origins created by the nizams in their royal kitchens.

But the real joys of Hyderabad are beyond the main attractions: get lost while searching for noble-family cemeteries still sprinkled daily with rose petals, ornate mosques and shrines tucked behind shopping plazas, garden complexes named for beloved courtesans, and neighbourhoods of fading mansions with centuries-old architectural flourishes.

FESTIVALS & EVENTS

✪ During January's Sankranti, everyone is either on their rooftops flying colourful kites

...WHAT'S NOT

Wearing shorts or tight T-shirts in the Old City, those new electronic autorickshaw meters, the city's Cinderella nightlife laws (clubs close at midnight)

HOT TOPIC OF THE DAY

For decades, a separatist movement has pushed to make Telangana – a region of Andhra Pradesh that includes Hyderabad – its own state. The debate grew heated in 2011–12, with mass strikes, fasts and political wrangling. Andhra's 'tribal' minorities, meanwhile, are still waiting for basic civil and property rights.

MOST BIZARRE SIGHT

The Charminar, a beautiful odd bird of a monument with 56m-high minarets, was built in 1591 to celebrate the city's founding. It's right in the middle of the Old City's busiest street and, though it has a mosque on its second floor, mostly exists just to be beautiful, especially when lit up at night.

CLASSIC RESTAURANT EXPERIENCE

The little local joint Hotel Shadab, at a chaotic intersection in the Old City, is full of friendly waiters, families and ladies who lunch (in black), and serves exquisite takes on traditional Old City cuisine.

BEST SHOPPING

In addition to too many megamalls, Hyderabad has the ancient and enthralling mall of Laad Bazaar – a vast labyrinth of vendors dealing in pearls, burqas, sequined slippers, tools, gems, bangles, fabrics and artisanal perfumes.

or observing the fluttering of thousands of kites against the skyline.

✪ Muharram, a 40-day festival commemorating the martyrdom of Mohammed's grandson, sees throngs of Hyderabadis coming together at mosques and shrines for prayer, processions and fire-walking.

✪ Serious evening eating happens during Ramadan, when the city lights up special clay ovens to make its famous *haleem* – pounded, spiced wheat mixed with goat or mutton.

WHAT'S HOT...

Designer Ritu Kumar's Falaknuma couture line (and the sari revival in general), gay pride, Hyderabad's nightlife and food scene

by Abigail Blasi

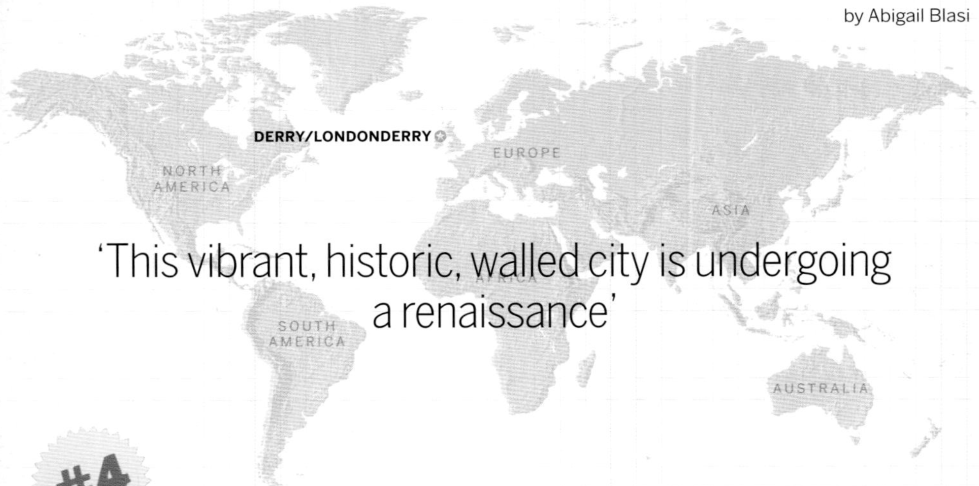

DERRY/LONDONDERRY

NORTH AMERICA

EUROPE

ASIA

SOUTH AMERICA

AUSTRALIA

'This vibrant, historic, walled city is undergoing a renaissance'

#4

EVENTS | CULTURE | FAMILY

DERRY/LONDONDERRY, NORTHERN IRELAND

- **POPULATION** 83,700
- **FOREIGN VISITORS PER YEAR** 278,141
- **LANGUAGES** English, Gaelic
- **UNIT OF CURRENCY** Pounds sterling (£)
- **COST INDEX** Pint of beer £3.30 (US$5.20), hotel double for a night from £50 (US$80), short taxi ride (minimum fare) £2.50 (US$4), wi-fi access per hour £1 (US$1.60)

WHY GO IN 2013? A YEAR IN THE LIMELIGHT

Derry/Londonderry is the UK City of Culture 2013, which means this vibrant, historic, walled city is undergoing a renaissance, despite a rocky reputation in the media. It's already gained a sinuous new foot and cycle bridge (the 235m 'Peace Bridge'), which forms an elegant wiggle across the River Doyle. The bridge symbolically links the city's Protestant and Catholic communities, and is designed to resemble a structural handshake.

The year will see a wealth of cultural events. The city will host the 10-day All Ireland Fleadh, the world's biggest Irish festival, which usually attracts around 300,000 visitors. The always-controversial Turner Prize will take place here, and other major art exhibitions include the best Magnum Photography and a show from the IMMA (Irish Museum of Modern Art).

Acclaimed Irish poet Paul Muldoon is writing a special piece to mark 400 years of the Derry walls along with the composer Mark Anthony Turnage, and the classical oratorio will debut in the Derry Guildhall and the London Guildhall simultaneously. Derry's famous fortifications will be further celebrated when Hofesh Schecter – the world's foremost young choreographer – stages a dance spectacular atop the walls.

The riverside Ebrington Barracks, to one side of the Peace Bridge, were once occupied by British troops. Today the former parade ground forms a performance space bigger than Trafalgar Square, with a contemporary art gallery in what was the headquarters building, a museum in the sometime military hospital, plus studios, cafes and bars.

The city will buzz throughout the year with hundreds of other events, from pageants to music to contemporary dance. Derry/Londonderry also hosts lots of regular festivals, such as the Jazz Festival and Earhart Festival (in 2013, celebrating 80 years since American aviation pioneer Amelia Earhart landed here), celebrations for which will all be cranked up a notch.

LIFE-CHANGING EXPERIENCE

Derry/Londonderry has a tumultuous history, and nothing illustrates this more movingly than the 12 murals that decorate the gable ends of houses along Rossville St, near Free Derry Corner. These are the work of the 'Bogside Artists': Tom Kelly, Will Kelly and Kevin Hasson. These three local men lived through the worst of the Troubles, and have poured their personal experience into the works, which are the city's most compelling and unusual sight.

FESTIVALS & EVENTS

✪ A huge pageant, with a cast of 2000, will take place on the river to celebrate St Colmcille on his feast day, 9 June.

RANDOM FACTS

✪ Derry/Londonderry is a town with three names. In the 10th century it was named Doíre Colmcille (Oak Grove of Columba), in honour of the 6th-century saint, so the Gaelic name is Doíre; Nationalists use Derry; and Unionists use Londonderry, which is still the city's official name. The 'London' part is often crossed out on the region's road signs.

✪ The Derry/Londonderry city walls were designed by Italian engineer Hieronimo Marino, who based their layout on the grid plan of a Roman military camp.

MOST BIZARRE SIGHT

Giant's Causeway, 64km eastward along the coast, is a collection of 40,000 interlocking ancient basalt columns created following volcanic action, the tops of which appear like sculpted stepping stones.

CLASSIC RESTAURANT EXPERIENCE

Housed over three floors of a handsome former shirt factory decorated with local art and photography, the Halo Pantry & Grill on Market St is held with great affection in town for its warm, New York–loft atmosphere, reasonable prices and lovely home-cooked food.

CLASSIC PLACE TO STAY

The Georgian Merchant's House is a grandiose townhouse, now a B&B, which transports you back to the elegance of 19th-century Derry, with its gracious drawing and dining rooms, polished woodwork, marble fireplaces, antique furniture, and homemade marmalade at breakfast.

✪ In mid-June, Foyle Days sees Derry/Londonderry take to the water for this river-based festival, featuring visiting navy ships, yacht races and boat trips, and shore-side music and entertainment.

✪ The Gasyard Wall Féile takes place in August with live music, street performers, theatre and Irish-language events.

✪ From 27 to 31 October, Derry gets over-excitedly spooky with the Halloween Carnival, Ireland's biggest street party.

HOT TOPIC OF THE DAY

Will Derry/Londonderry's status as European Capital of Culture help to bridge the gaps between Protestants and Catholics?

by Shawn Low

NORTH
AMERICA

EUROPE

● BEIJING

ASIA

'...the entire city feels like the Wild West meets circa-1980s Tokyo meets, well, modern-day China'

AMERICA

AUSTRALIA

#5

VALUE CULTURE FOOD

BEIJING, CHINA

- ✪ **POPULATION** 19.6 million
- ✪ **VISITORS PER YEAR** 4.9 million
- ✪ **LANGUAGE** Mandarin
- ✪ **UNIT OF CURRENCY** Chinese renminbi (RMB) also referred to as the yuan (Y)
- ✪ **COST INDEX** Bottle of Tsingtao beer Y15 (US$2.30), hotel double room per night Y400-2500 (US$64-400), dorm bed per night Y100-150 (US$16-24), short taxi ride Y18 (US$2.80), admission to the Forbidden City Y40-60 (US$6-10), Peking duck meal at Quanjude Restaurant Y170 (US$27)

WHY GO 2013? BEIJING – BIGGER AND BETTER

Shanghai may be flaunting its financial cred (yawn), but Beijing firmly remains as the cultural and artistic centre of China. While the 2008 Olympics may now seem like a distant memory, its effect is enduring – there are English street signs and a multitude of architectural gems such as the Bird's Nest studded across the sprawling city. More recently, the Beijing–Shanghai high-speed rail now connects the two cities in under five hours.

Today, Beijing tentatively balances a multitude of (growing) populations and subcultures. Expats number in the hundreds of thousands, migrants from around China come to seek their fortunes here, and the entire city feels like the Wild West meets circa-1980s Tokyo meets, well, modern-day China. While the classical sights such as Tiananmen Square, the Forbidden City, the Great Wall and the Summer Palace remain as they've always been, there's a plethora of varied activities coming to a boil in Beijing.

Artist colonies have sprung up in Caochangdi (Ai Weiwei instigated the move here) and Songzhuang (more than 2000 artists), while the city's growing alternative rock and punk scene rocks local clubs. Sitting somewhat uneasily beside this is China's largest nouveau-riche population, with their Ferraris and penchant for Hermès and Chateau Margaux. Beijing truly is the sum of its disparate parts. There's a palpable

LING JIAN'S EXHIBITION, MOON IN GLASS, AT THE ULLENS CENTER FOR CONTEMPORARY ART, BEIJING

sense of change in the air, though no one quite knows what to expect. China is on the cusp of true greatness and one day, people will look back and say it all started here.

LIFE-CHANGING EXPERIENCES

Get a kick walking through the huge double doors into the Forbidden City – the pièce de résistance of China experiences – and it's not an easy feat to stand out in the world's third-largest country. At night, let a local punk rock band set your ears ringing while you chug back Tsingtao at the wildly popular MAO Livehouse. Recharge on street snacks such as fried scorpion, stinky tofu and spicy pancakes before clambering along the less-touristy Jiankou and Simatai sections of the Great Wall and doing something crazy on it (marathon? camping? Take your pick).

FESTIVALS & EVENTS

✪ Nerds, bibliophiles and intellectuals come together in March for the Beijing Bookworm International Literary Festival. For details, visit www.bookwormfestival.com.
✪ Each May, fitness freaks get a kick out of running a marathon... on the Great Wall!

The route goes over some steep ascents, up and down thousands of steps and through local villages. Check out www.great-wall-marathon.com.

✪ While the rave party on the Great Wall has been banned, organisers have managed to keep shenanigans going by having an annual rave party on the beach in the Shanhaiguan section – where the wall meets the sea. Come July, locals and expats don their swimsuits for a bit of hedonistic partying at the Great Wall Beach Party. Book at www.greatwallbeachparty.com. So, can you wear a bikini? The organiser's FAQ says, quite emphatically, 'Yes!'.

WHAT'S HOT...
Caochangdi Art District, obscure *hutong* (alleyways), cycling

...WHAT'S NOT
Boorish expats, traffic jams, sandstorms

MOST BIZARRE SIGHT
The embalmed body of Chairman Mao lies in a crystal cabinet in a mausoleum complex at – where else – Tiananmen Square. White-gloved guards wave the crowds along to the souvenir shop stocked with Mao memorabilia. Lines snake out the main entrance and locals adopt an air of almost religious reverence when in the presence of China's late statesman... so no giggling here.

CLASSIC RESTAURANT EXPERIENCE
It may be a cliché, but you have to sample Peking duck in Beijing. The Beijing Dadong Roast Duck Restaurant is a long-time favourite and its popularity is certainly warranted. The air-conditioned setting may lack atmosphere, but it serves up a yummy lean version (15% fat versus the normal 42%) of the fowl complete with plum sauce, scallions and pancakes. For a decidedly more low-key experience, visit the grungy Li Qun Roast Duck Restaurant, run out of a traditional courtyard house. The mighty oven stands in the courtyard, turning out perfectly crisp-skinned ducks.

BEST SHOPPING
For a big-city shopping experience, take a stroll along Wangfujing Dajie, home to malls, malls, malls. The trendy set hang out at Sanlitun for its luxury brands – though pirate DVD stalls are often tucked across the street. The *hutong* (alleyways) of Dashilar are a jumble of silk shops, old stores selling bric-a-brac, and herbal medicine shops (dried starfish anyone?). For antiques and curios, drop by Panjiayuan Market on the weekends. Up to 50,000 people rummage for calligraphy, Cultural Revolution memorabilia, Tibetan carpets, vintage furniture and everything in between. Bargain hard as some mark-ups are said to be 10 times the selling price!

CLASSIC PLACE TO STAY
Beijing's fast-disappearing courtyard houses provide great settings for some fabulous boutique hotels. Courtyard 7 (www.courtyard7.com) has traditional rosewood-furnished rooms spread out across three lovely buildings. Also try Mao'er 28 (www.maoer28.com), often booked out a year in advance.

by Craig McLachlan

'...Christchurch, with a unique opportunity to rethink urban form, is bouncing back with a new energy and inventiveness'

CHRISTCHURCH

#6

CHRISTCHURCH, NEW ZEALAND

EVENTS | CULTURE | FAMILY

- ✪ **POPULATION** 380,000
- ✪ **FOREIGN VISITORS PER YEAR** 70,000
- ✪ **LANGUAGE** English
- ✪ **UNIT OF CURRENCY** New Zealand dollar ($)
- ✪ **COST INDEX** Pint of beer $7 (US$6), dorm room per night $30 (US$24), short taxi ride $15 (US$12), hassle-free city tour $29 (US$23), admission to Antarctic Centre $35 (US$28)

WHY GO IN 2013? SOAK IN THE ENERGY OF THE REBUILD

New Zealand's second-largest city is rising from the rubble created by devastating earthquakes in 2010 and 2011 with a breathtaking mix of spirit, determination and flair. Half the city centre was knocked over and 185 lives were lost, but Christchurch, with a unique opportunity to rethink urban form, is bouncing back with a new energy and inventiveness. In the city itself, exciting things are going on. Foodies will be surprised by the variety of what is on offer, from Burmese to Turkish to local specialities, live-music venues have popped up all over the place, and innovative artworks fill empty demolition sites. Who would have believed that the humble shipping container would emerge as a funky option for housing everything from noodle bars to book shops and fashion boutiques? Meanwhile, the recovery effort is well under way and 2013 will be an intriguing year to join the rebirth of this proud southern city.

Christchurch's CBD may have taken a hit but nearby hotspots such as Akaroa, Hanmer Springs, Kaikoura, Mt Hutt and the Southern Alps were relatively untouched by the quakes, and remain fantastic options for side-trips from Christchurch.

THE RAKAIA RIVER
FLOWS ACROSS THE
CANTERBURY PLAINS,
CLOSE TO CHRISTCHURCH

LIFE-CHANGING EXPERIENCES

While the earthquakes and aftershocks provided plenty of life-changing and nerve-rattling experiences for the locals, the resilience and determination they displayed has helped bind the people of the Canterbury region together. The 'Farmy Army' descended on the city from the region's rural heartland with shovels and food hampers, social media mobilised a 10,000-strong Student Volunteer Army for clean-up action, and heartfelt aid arrived from across New Zealand and around the globe.

Expect a warm welcome. Locals, while still hurting, are fighting back, and the energy of the rebuilding effort is sure to rub off on visitors. This is drive and determination at its best. Marvel at the 'cardboard cathedral', the stunning inspiration of Japanese architect Shigeru Ban, which will replace the city's iconic stone cathedral. The 700-seat transitional cathedral, built of durable cardboard tubes, to be completed in December 2012, is expected to serve the city for the next 20 years.

FESTIVALS & EVENTS

✪ The World Buskers Festival hits Christchurch in mid to late January with entertainers from far and wide enthralling passers-by on city streets.
✪ The Garden City comes alive for the Festival of Flowers and Ellerslie Flower Show in February and March. Be part of a blooming spectacle.
✪ In November, the NZ Cup and Show Week includes the NZ Cup horse race, complete with best-dressed fashion competitions and the centrepiece A&P (Agricultural & Pastoral) Show.

RECENT FAD

The Gap Filler Charitable Trust is filling the gaps left at empty demolition sites with creative projects such as the Lyttleton Petanque Club, the 'Think Differently Book Exchange' (a fridge crammed with books), giant chess boards for the public to use, and all sorts of artworks and performances. Some of the 'gaps' being used are semipermanent, some are only available for a few days.

HOT TOPIC OF THE DAY

What's opening today? Christchurch is buzzing with positivity and constantly evolving. Everyone wants to keep up to date with new openings and reopenings. Check out Pop-Up City (www.popupcity.co.nz).

MOST BIZARRE SIGHT

The Re:START development on Cashel Mall sees retailers back in action on the fringe of the CBD in a colourful labyrinth of shipping containers. Besides the opportunity for some retail therapy, free wi-fi and alfresco cafes help provide a distraction from the hustle and bustle of demolition and rebuilding.

CLASSIC RESTAURANT EXPERIENCE

Captain Cook may have called it the 'tea tree' and used its leaves to brew tea, but at Holy Smoke (www.holysmoke.co.nz) on Ferry Rd they use the manuka tree's wood to smoke everything from pork ribs and salmon to garlic! This multi-award-winning place also serves up local craft beers and top NZ wines to give you a unique Christchurch and Kiwi dining experience.

by Kate Morgan

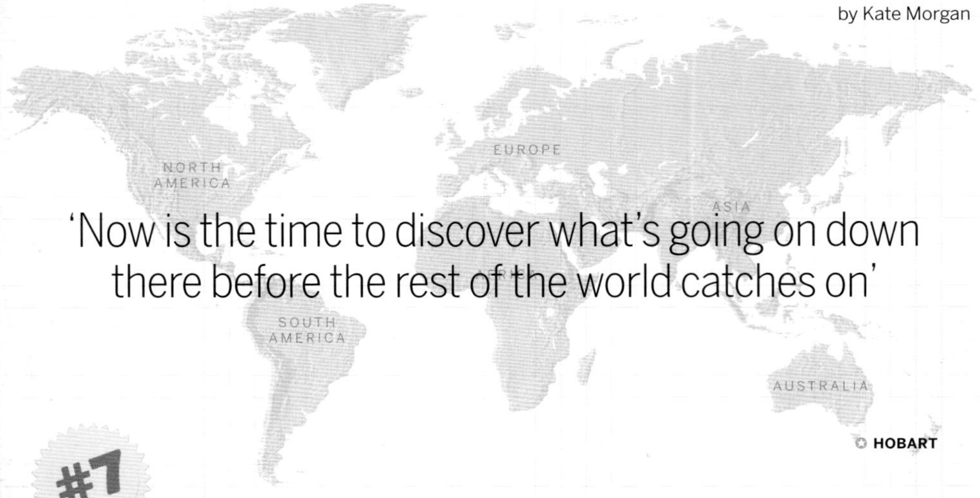

NORTH
AMERICA

EUROPE

ASIA

'Now is the time to discover what's going on down
there before the rest of the world catches on'

SOUTH
AMERICA

AUSTRALIA

◌ HOBART

#7

EVENTS   CULTURE   FOOD

HOBART, AUSTRALIA

- ✪ **POPULATION** 214,000
- ✪ **FOREIGN VISITORS PER YEAR** 112,000
- ✪ **LANGUAGE** English
- ✪ **UNIT OF CURRENCY** Australian dollar ($)
- ✪ **COST INDEX** Coffee $3.50 (US$3.60), meal in a restaurant $20-25 (US$21-26), MONA art museum admission $20 (US$21), midrange hotel double $140-180 (US$145-186), schooner of Cascade beer $6 (US$6.20)

WHY GO IN 2013? A HISTORIC CITY REINVENTING ITSELF

Resting on the banks of the Derwent River against the backdrop of Mt Wellington, Hobart's allure has always been its natural beauty. A sleepy reputation attracts a solid 'outdoorsy' set dressed in the obligatory fleece and boat shoes, but the recent arrival of the world-class MONA museum has the waters rippling, hip tourists flocking and Hobart rousing from its slumber.

MONA is Australia's largest private art museum, housing the $150 million collection of its eccentric owner, David Walsh, in a subterranean space built into the sandstone banks of the Derwent. In 2013 the new kid on the block will team up with the Tasmanian Museum and Art Gallery (TMAG) for the Theatre of the World exhibition curated by Jean-Hubert Martin, former director of the Centre Georges Pompidou in Paris. Not to be outdone by MONA, TMAG will be getting a significant makeover – to be revealed in early 2013 – that will see spaces previously off limits to the public showing off a suite of new exhibitions and heritage works.

And since the art revival began, a free bicycle-hire service, Artbikes, has been set up for visitors to access the city's art trails and there's a map to guide you to Hobart's best galleries.

This year will also prove exciting for Hobart's already burgeoning gastronomic scene as the city's culinary credentials continue to rise. A focus on organic,

sustainable and biodynamic ingredients is an emerging theme (particularly with restaurants Garagistes and Ethos), boutique microbreweries are popping up, Salamanca Market and Farm Gate Market continue to show off the regional produce and city food tours have also taken off. Now is the time to discover what's going on down there before the rest of the world catches on.

LIFE-CHANGING EXPERIENCE

Australia's second-oldest city, Hobart is steeped in history and not an altogether pleasant one. Take in the Louisa's Walk tour for an informative insight into the infamous Female Factory where female convicts were incarcerated. If your newfound knowledge of this chilling past has you rattled, head over to the Lark Distillery for one of their whisky tours and end it with a smooth single malt to get you back on track.

FESTIVALS & EVENTS

✪ Ex-Violent Femmes bassist, Brian Ritchie, curates MONA FOMA, a music/arts festival in January. Past performers include the Saints, John Cale and Grandmaster Flash.

✪ The biannual visual arts festival, Ten Days on the Island, runs in March and draws talent from all disciplines including dance, theatre, installation and literature.

✪ One for the boaters, the famous Sydney to Hobart Yacht Race sees yachts finishing this race around 29 December; the celebrations last for days.

✪ Hobart's waterfront is transformed into a feast for foodies from December through January where the fine Tassie produce is on show at the popular Taste Festival.

RANDOM FACTS

❂ The last known living Tasmanian tiger died in captivity at the Hobart Zoo in 1936.
❂ Errol Flynn and the Crown Princess of Denmark were born-and-bred Hobartians.
❂ Hobart is home to Australia's oldest brewery, Cascade Brewery, established in 1824 and still in operation.

WHAT'S HOT...

MONA, of course. So hot that Hobart's recent tourism boom is referred to as 'the MONA effect' (in its first year, the museum attracted almost half a million visitors).

...WHAT'S NOT

The weather – Hobart has a deserved reputation for having more than its fair share of wet days and frosty Antarctic winds.

CLASSIC RESTAURANT EXPERIENCE

Housed in an old mechanics garage, the star of the growing dining scene is Garagistes, with a menu that respects the land and the sea using locally grown and foraged ingredients. Tetsuya-trained chef, Luke Burgess, dishes up innovative fare such as chawan-mushi and spanner crab with dashi poached onions. It's not all about the food here though: organic or biodynamic wine is the focus and food is served to match, rather than vice-versa.

CLASSIC PLACE TO STAY

The Islington Hotel, a grand historic residence in manicured gardens, was built in 1847 as a hotel and still houses many southbound visitors today. It is filled with antiques, artefacts and contemporary art.

by Caroline Veldhuis

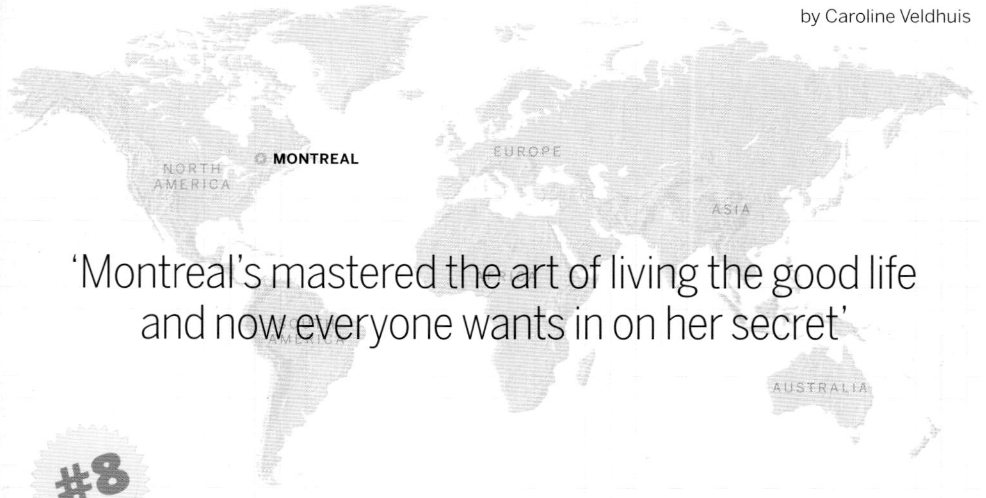

NORTH AMERICA ● MONTREAL EUROPE ASIA AUSTRALIA

'Montreal's mastered the art of living the good life and now everyone wants in on her secret'

#8

VALUE   EVENTS   CULTURE

MONTREAL, CANADA

- ✪ **POPULATION** 3.8 million
- ✪ **FOREIGN VISITORS PER YEAR** 7 million
- ✪ **LANGUAGES** French (official), English widely spoken
- ✪ **UNIT OF CURRENCY** Canadian dollar ($)
- ✪ **COST INDEX** Cup of coffee $2 (US$2), bottle of wine from the SAQ $10-20 (US$10-20), midrange hotel double $90-150 (US$90-150), short taxi ride $10-15 (US$10-15), Schwartz's Deli sandwich $6.20 (US$6.20), poutine $4-8 (US$$4-8), Musée des Beaux-Arts permanent collection free

MONTREAL'S BIOSPHÈRE MUSEUM ON ÎLE SAINTE-HÉLÈNE ISLAND

WHY GO IN 2013? BECAUSE SHE'S ON EVERYONE'S LIPS

Like the girl everyone wants to go out with, Montreal has a confidence that has always attracted people in droves. She's mastered the art of living the good life and now everyone wants in on her secret. Having recently gained a high rank on city lists including the world's happiest (Lonely Planet, 2010) and hippest (*New York Times*, 2011), this year she's angling for a top spot, showing off in Steven Spielberg's summer release *Robopocalypse*, and inviting everyone for drinks at the new urban beach.

But Montreal's making sure we know she's got brains as well as beauty. Spring 2013 marks the launch of the new Rio Tinto Alcan Planetarium, rounding out the ambitious 'Space for Life' project, a natural-science extravaganza that includes the extant and mammoth-sized Biodôme, Insectarium and Botanical Garden. A model for architectural sustainability, the planetarium features two conical theatres for space education and a green roof that visitors can even walk on.

Montreal's social calendar is also bubbling over with the unveiling of the Grévin wax museum at the Eaton Centre (at twice the size of the original in Paris), the 50th-anniversary celebrations of the Place des Arts, and the new Point Zero hotel, owned by the eponymous fashion label.

And what of the endless quarrel between this French style maven and the pesky Anglophones? These days a whiff of libertarianism is breezing through a heady mélange of cultures. More universal concerns like food and water are soaking up Montreal's energy. It's turning into a bit of a love-fest all around, and everyone is invited.

LIFE-CHANGING EXPERIENCES

Part of the urban dream and the city's namesake, the hills of Mt Royal require no training to summit and it's magical in winter: squirrels dart across the path as you zoom up and around the trees on cross-country skis or snowshoes. Take in the spectacular cityscape and a glimpse of the St Lawrence at the Kondiaronk Belvedere lookout. Then head down to tuck into the Québec comfort food that has become de rigeur: *tourtière*, maple-syrup soaked *pudding au chômeur* (poor man's pudding) and an ice cider.

FESTIVALS & EVENTS

✪ Canada Snow Village, in the Parc Jean-Drapeau, is a frozen spectacle that runs from January through March and includes a spa, ice hotel, bar, five-star restaurant and chapel; 2013's theme is New York.
✪ The Festival Mondial de la Bière in May/June features more than 500 beers, including local microbrews: it's Oktoberfest with a French twist.
✪ A three-day celebration of wheels, Montreal Bike Fest in May/June includes a 50-km day tour and Friday-night ride through the city.

RECENT FAD

Now you see it, now you don't: 'pop-up' shops, galleries and restaurants have been popping up all around town.

WHAT'S HOT...

Socially responsible businesses, Little Italy, Italian food, Italians, winter

...WHAT'S NOT

Homelessness, climate change

HOT TOPIC OF THE DAY

Two icons met up and made headlines when songstress Celine Dion and husband Rene Angelil were recently named in a group that bought Schwartz's Deli — adding to their stock of restaurants, which includes the local diner chain Nickels. Is one of Montreal's favourite landmarks destined to become a Las Vegas–style franchise? The celebs are saying no... let's hold them to it.

MOST BIZARRE SIGHT

Visitors are occasionally bewildered to encounter the Tam Tams on summer Sunday afternoons in Mount Royal Park: a congregation of drummers and dancers that may well be the beating heart of the city. Remember this was where John Lennon and Yoko Ono held a love-in...

BEST SHOPPING

Minimalist classics, plus recycled wear, plus Québec-designed leather bags and accessories equals Montreal chic. Pair locally produced, ecofriendly Second Denim jeans with a jacket or knitwear from Preloved. Visit Rudsak, M0851 and Want les Essentiels de la Vie for leather accoutrements that will give your look that *je ne sais quoi* long after you've returned home.

by Jean-Bernard Carillet

'....the Merkato is lined with stalls and shops, where you can buy anything from Kakashnikovs and camels to spices and jewellery'

○ **ADDIS ABABA**

#9

ADDIS ABABA, ETHIOPIA

VALUE   CULTURE   FOOD

- ❂ **POPULATION** 3 million
- ❂ **FOREIGN VISITORS PER YEAR** around 50,000
- ❂ **LANGUAGE** Amharic
- ❂ **UNIT OF CURRENCY** Ethiopian birr (ETB)
- ❂ **COST INDEX** Cup of macchiato birr4 (US$0.22), cover charge at a disco birr50 (US$2.80), double room in a midrange hotel from birr700 (US$40), traditional meal at a reputable restaurant birr120 (US$6.75)

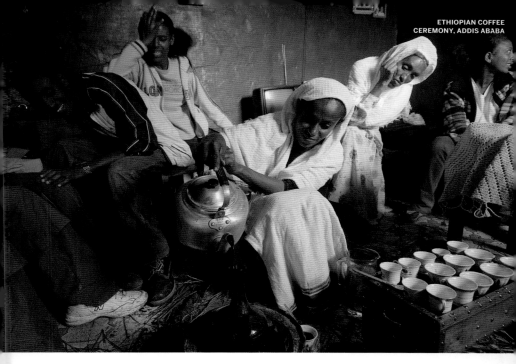

WHY GO?
A BLOSSOMING FLOWER

Like the Ethiopian marathon runners, Addis Ababa (often shortened to plain Addis) is evolving at a fast pace. The fact that the country's economic growth should reach almost 5% in 2013 helps create a feeling of confidence and stamina. Founded little more than a century ago, Addis Ababa, which in Amharic means 'New Flower', is not only the diplomatic capital of Africa and a thriving metropolis, but also a groovy city that takes pride in its multifaceted assets. Perched on the Abyssinian plateau, some 2400m above sea level, Addis boasts a climate classed as 'tropical highland'; in other words, balmy and temperate, with cloudless blue skies for about eight months of the year – all the more reason to visit. It's well endowed with museums, including the culturally stimulating Ethnological Museum, set within Emperor Haile Selassie's former palace, which gives a great insight into Ethiopia's many rich cultures. Another highlight is the National Museum, the collection of which ranks among the finest in sub-Saharan Africa; its star attraction is Lucy, the oldest hominid ever found by archaeologists. Addis also gets rave reviews for its restaurant scene and nightlife. Bole Road – the avenue that connects the airport to the centre – is the fashionable district, with plenty of fancy bars, eateries, galleries and clubs. Addis

BRIGHT LIGHTS, BRILLIANT CITY:
ADDIS ABABA BY NIGHT

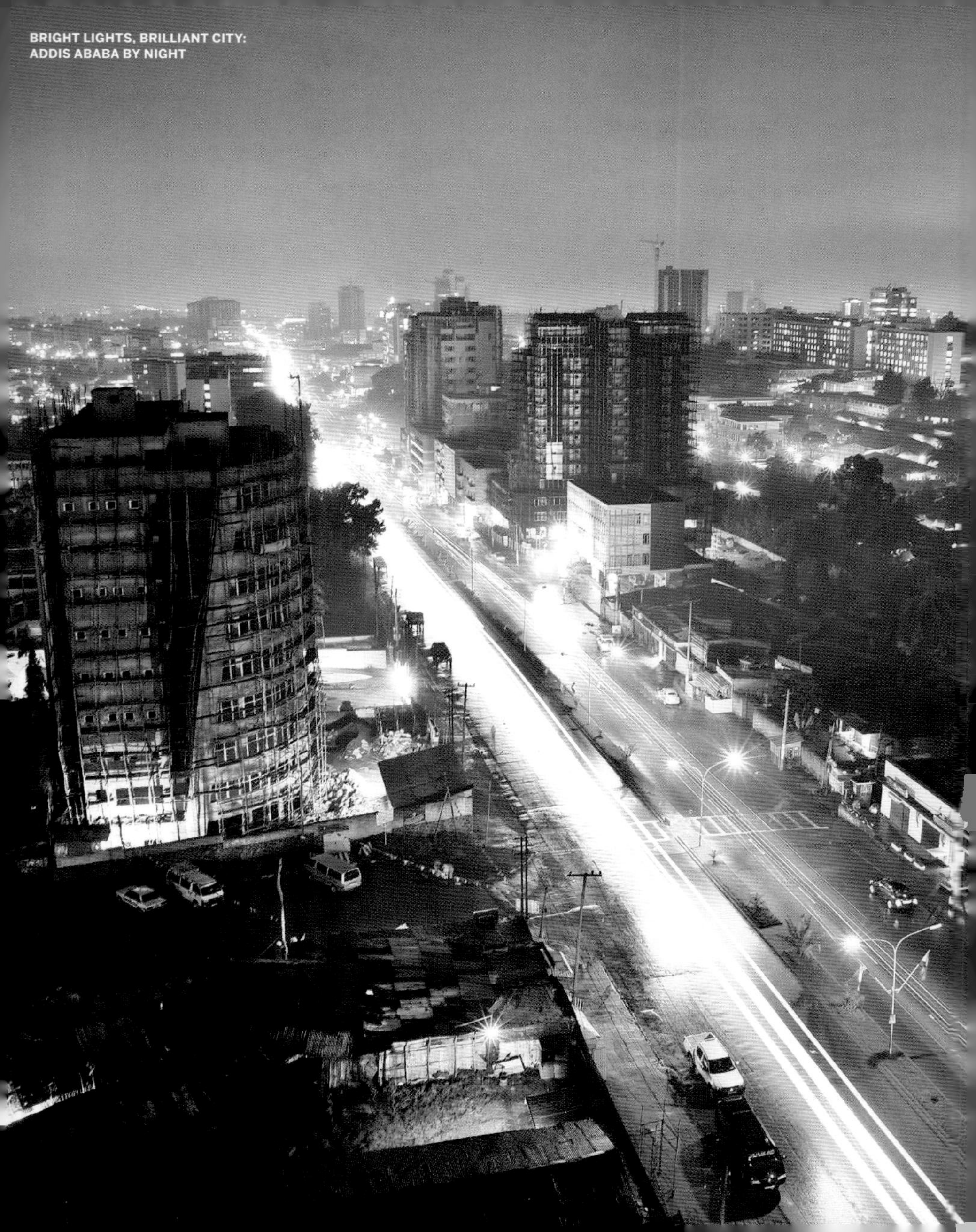

has lots of great surprises up its sleeve – it's time to delve in!

LIFE-CHANGING EXPERIENCE
A few hours spent wandering the alleys of the sprawling, open-air Merkato is an experience you won't forget. East Africa's largest market, it is a grid of roads lined with stalls and small shops, where you can buy anything you want, from Kakashnikovs and camels to spices and jewellery. Be prepared for a sensory overload.

FESTIVALS & EVENTS
✪ The 10km Great Ethiopian Run takes over the city on the last Sunday of November. With more than 20,000 runners, it's the biggest mass-participation race in Africa.
✪ During the Ethiopian Orthodox festival of Leddet (6 and 7 January), priests don their full regalia and the faithful attend all-night church services. Horse races and traditional games, such as *genna* (a kind of hockey), are also organised.
✪ Less than two weeks after Leddet, on 19 January, Timkat (Epiphany) is another highly colourful religious festival. Dressed in white, the monks march in procession and dance.

RANDOM FACTS
✪ At an altitude of 2400m, Addis Ababa is the world's third-highest capital city.
✪ The city's largest square, Meskal Square, is where runners jog every morning before dawn. The country's elite marathon runners can be seen training in the windy Entoto Mountains, on the capital's northern outskirts.

✪ *Tej beat* (pronounced 'tedj bet') are specialist bars that focus on serving *tej,* the powerful local mead brewed from honey. *Tej beats* are the traditional haunts of men.
✪ The Holy Trinity Cathedral is the final resting place of Emperor Haile Selassie, who is buried in the church grounds.

MOST BIZARRE SIGHT
Meet your long-lost Auntie Lucy, our common ancestor, in Addis. The remains of this fossilised hominid woman were discovered in 1974 in Ethiopia's northeast and are now conserved in the National Museum. What you can actually see consists of two casts – one lays prone, while the other stands much like she did 3.2 million years ago.

HOT TOPIC OF THE DAY
When will a final peace agreement with Eritrea be reached? For more than two decades, tensions have been high between Ethiopia and its neighbour over the demarcation border.

CLASSIC RESTAURANT EXPERIENCE
For newcomers to Ethiopian fare, Habesha Restaurant is the perfect venue to get an initiation in local specialities, such as *zilzil tibs* (marinated beef cooked on clay) or *doro wat* (chicken drumstick or wing in a hot sauce). After your meal, indulge in the coffee ceremony. The coffee is served in small china cups; at least three cups must be accepted. The interior is lush, with scattered low tables and assorted indoor spaces, and the atmosphere is great, with traditional music most evenings.

by Luke Waterson

'It might not quite be El Dorado, but it's fair to say that despite its popular waterfalls, Iguazú is still an undiscovered treasure'

○ **PUERTO IGUAZÚ**

#10

PUERTO IGUAZÚ, ARGENTINA

ACTIVITIES | ADVENTURE | FAMILY

- ○ **POPULATION** 82,000
- ○ **FOREIGN VISITORS PER YEAR** 1.1 million
- ○ **LANGUAGE** Spanish
- ○ **UNIT OF CURRENCY** Argentine peso (A$)
- ○ **COST INDEX** Mixed grill for two with bottle of Malbec A$150 (US$35), midrange hotel double/hostel dorm A$90/40 (US$20/9), Foz de Iguazú entrance fee A$130 (US$30)

WHY GO IN 2013? FALLING HEAD OVER HEELS

It's official: votes are in and the Foz de Iguazú has won its place among the prestigious new seven wonders of nature, following a worldwide 2011 poll. That this waterfall, spreadeagled along the Argentine–Brazil border, should make the final reckoning of nature's most enthralling sights is no great shock. The stats speak volumes: higher, wider and with several times the flow capacity of Niagara Falls, 275 separate cataracts tumble 80m through jungle in a body of water more than 2km across.

So tourism to the falls is set to morph, which is good news for Puerto Iguazú, the main tourist base hereabouts. The town, Argentina's most northeasterly and known to locals as 'Iguazú', is used to others waxing lyrical about its nearby star attraction well before the town gets so much as a mention, but it doesn't *just* want to be the fall guy. After all, Puerto Iguazú offers some of the best hostels, top-end hotels and spas in the country. The lavish Iguazú Grand picked up 'Argentina's best resort' at the 2011 World Travel Awards and the other fancy digs in town, the Sheraton Iguazú, has just been refurbished. And, almost as refreshing as a dunk in the Devil's Throat (that's the Falls' most gargantuan cataract), local tourism agencies are finally featuring trips to the stunning Wanda mines, one of the continent's most important gem deposits, on the itineraries. It might not quite be El Dorado, but it's fair to say that despite its popular waterfalls, Iguazú is still a largely undiscovered treasure.

LIFE-CHANGING EXPERIENCES

Iguazú is a growing honeymoon and casino-holiday destination, but you don't have to be a love bird to get passionate about the place. Visits to the nearby waterfalls on both the Argentine and Brazilian sides are essential: take a boat trip under the biggest cascades or a helicopter ride over them. And, in a surrounding jungle featuring some 2000 plant species and animals such as jaguars, it's worth exploring away from the water. If possible, splash out accommodation-wise in Iguazú (the Sheraton has the best waterfall views) for some of the most sublime hotel experiences Argentina offers. But the backpacking scene is as buoyant as they come, and Iguazú's renowned social life enhances chances for travellers to seek kindred spirits. A night at the Tres Fronteras (three frontiers) nightclub, at the point where Argentina, Brazil and Paraguay meet, is a must-do for nightlife-lovers. Representatives of each nation start the night in separate corners and, as the alcohol flows, start mingling with the flip-flop–clad gringos. Return by the subtropical light of day for cross-river views where the Iguazú and Parana converge: at the point where the borders touch, the three countries have erected respective obelisks prettily decorated in their national colours.

FESTIVALS & EVENTS

✪ May's Iguazú en Concierto (Iguazú in concert) is probably the biggest youth-orchestra event on the planet, with performances in the top hotels and against a waterfall backdrop.

✪ On Brazil's side of the Falls in Foz de Iguaçu, June sees the Festival do Turismo das Cataratas (tourism festival of the falls), showcasing tourism across Mercosur countries Argentina, Brazil, Paraguay and Uruguay. Look out too for the special emphasis on the cuisine and customs of southernmost Brazil.

RANDOM FACTS

✪ The Falls have been deemed exotic and otherworldly enough to have featured in James Bond and Indiana Jones films.
✪ Iguazú sits on the Guarani Aquifer, the world's biggest body of groundwater.
✪ According to legend, Foz de Iguazú was created when a god coveted a local woman who chose to flee with her lover downriver instead. The nasty god split the river; the lovers got consigned to falling for eternity.

CLASSIC RESTAURANT EXPERIENCE

If your taste buds are whetted for food few foreigners find, head to Iguazú's *feria* (market). There you'll find little Recanto Argentino (translating as Argentine hidden place), a humble but renowned booth staying open late for wine (get the Malbec) and gorgeous platters of cured meats, cheese and olives.

CLASSIC PLACE TO STAY

Lovingly restored Panoramic Hotel Iguazú is the least-known luxury hotel, but with its 1940s architecture and infinity pool overlooking the river-flanked tri-border, it could be top dog for ambience.

LONELY PLANET'S
TOP TRAVEL
LISTS

BEST-VALUE

SAVOUR EVERY CENTIMETRE OF THAT SHOESTRING WITH THESE
BUDGET-FRIENDLY BOLTHOLES, PERFECT FOR AN ECONOMIC
DOWNTURN-BUSTING BREAK.

o1 RIO, BRAZIL

If you've an unfulfilled plan to visit Rio de Janeiro's beaches and iconic landmarks then this may be the year to do it. After 2013 the big events come thick and fast – the football World Cup in 2014 (also taking place in cities around Brazil), then the Olympic Games in 2016. One thing's for sure: big-name events bring fresh development, a boost to infrastructure and, in many cases, higher prices for visitors. Come now to see a city in the process of gearing up to welcome the world, but before the costs of doing so rise. Indeed, if you visit during June you can be among the first to check out the recently upgraded Estádio do Maracanã, the world-famous venue that is slated to host not only the World Cup final in 2014 but also the opening and closing ceremonies of the Olympics and Paralympics.

02 GOTHENBURG, SWEDEN

There's good value in Sweden if you know where to look. That said, if you don't, even popping out for a pizza and beer can make for a pricey night by your home town's standards. Unless you're from Norway. Either way, the savvy traveller makes tracks for Gothenburg. Away from the glitzy main drag, Kungsportsavenyn (referred to as Avenyn by everyone), are character-filled neighbourhoods (hello, Haga and, a little outside town, Kvarnbyn), cheap eats and some great attractions, including edgy art space Röda Sten and picnic-friendly city views in Keillers Park. If that wasn't enough, ferries trundling round the beautiful, car-free southern archipelago are a tram ride from the city centre. In short, this is as much Scandinavia as you can get for your money.

03 CAMBODIA

While not the whoops-of-delight-inducing bargain it was a decade ago, Cambodia is still a great deal. Despite the boom in the number of midrange hotels in Phnom Penh and Siem Reap in particular, a huge amount of budget accommodation remains at lower prices. The imaginative visitor to the country exploring less-well-visited parts will find it easy to afford that extra Angkor beer or three. A budget of US$15 is tight but achievable, provided you forgo a room with air-con and don't dwell for too long in the headline destinations.

✪ BOLIVIA

South America's best-value option continues to delight travellers. With public transport as cheap as anywhere on the continent, filling street food (another empanada? Don't mind if I do!), and good-for-the-money excursions, this country is more than a bridge between the east and west coasts, it is an essential journey in itself. True, things are a little more expensive in La Paz and must-visit Uyuni, but away from here set-menu meals will rarely tip over US$5, budget rooms are not much more than double that and, should the chilly Altiplano nights require a higher standard of accommodation, you may find that you still leave for a pricier neighbourhood with a smile on your face.

✪ SPAIN

Spain has been getting much friendlier for budget travellers in the past few years, as currency fluctuations and falling costs for many items have combined to make what was once Europe's best bet for a cheap break a contender once again for many international travellers. Presumably if you're reading this you're not really the fly-and-flop type, but the wonders of Spain's cities, wilder north coast and fabulous national parks are more affordable now than for the past few years. To make your money go as far as possible anywhere in Spain, live without a pool, go easy on the wine and extra courses when eating out, and visit outside peak season, when price hikes remain.

✪ SLOVENIA

It's tempting to leave this as one sentence: Slovenia is as picture-perfect as Switzerland or any other northerly Alpine area, but much smaller and easier on the wallet. Yes, there's devil in the detail – the adoption of the euro and popularity of Ljubljana, Bled and coastal areas in summer can push prices up – but that's hardly the point. Small distances keep travel costs down, and buses radiating out of Ljubljana are plentiful and inexpensive. Private rooms offer affordable accommodation and anyone arriving from Austria or Italy will notice the difference in hotel prices at all budgets. If you're keen on trekking, skiing, rafting or simply taking in the scenery of one of Europe's most attractive countries then Slovenia will not disappoint.

✪ NEPAL

With visitor numbers rising, Nepal remains a tremendous option for budget travellers. After all, the number of countries where you can live on the price of a Starbucks latte or two are diminishing rapidly. Sure, to do that you'll need to stay in budget accommodation somewhere other than Kathmandu and resolutely stick to simple local food, but many consider this a price worth paying. Though costs rise once you enter national parks, if you're up for trekking on your own and staying in teahouses, Nepal is not only the best-value spot for Himalayan hiking, it must be a contender for offering the most astonishing rewards for the least upfront investment of anywhere in the world. This is true even if you factor in a porter and guide and opt for an organised trek.

✪ PORTLAND, OREGON, USA

Travel writers speak with one voice when asked to nominate their fave US cheapie: Portland, OR. Cheap food! Free things to do! Free light rail and streetcar services in the city centre! Forty breweries (and counting) with pints of perfectly crafted beer often costing US$4! Yes, budget-conscious but still fashionably minded travellers may have reached the promised land in Portland, Oregon. The city has been thrust into the limelight by the *Portlandia* TV series, but was hardly unknown before, offering as it does a progressive take on urban life in a part of the Pacific Northwest that's best appreciated slowly.

✪ GEORGIA

Georgia is, like its Caucasian neighbours, little known to most travellers. Those who go come back raving about a beautiful, friendly country offering excellent, inexpensive (though potentially waist-expanding) cuisine, typified by the near-universal *khachapuri* (cheese pie). Recently, the country has been speeding up its tourism development, resulting in a growing number of good-value hostels and homestays – great ways to meet locals, as well as keep costs down. Look out for August if you're hitting Batumi or elsewhere on the Black Sea coast, but otherwise anytime is a good time to visit this up-and-coming destination where even a bus, train or *marshrustka* minibus ride will give jaw-dropping views worth far more than the meagre fare you're likely to be charged.

✪ NAMIBIA

Namibia beckons those in search of a good deal. While neighbouring Botswana courts the big-budget traveller, the desert state to the west welcomes all, and offers a spectacular set of attractions to boot. True, you need your own wheels or must join a tour to see some of the wonders on offer, such as Etosha National Park and the Skeleton Coast, but Namibia's big-ticket draws remain affordable for budget and midrange visitors via locally arranged tours or self-drive car hire. Towns and cities, many offering keenly priced hostels and campsites, are linked by inexpensive buses and minivans. Some of the most fun things you can do here – sandboarding around Swakopmund and hiking Fish River Canyon, for instance – are also some of the best-value outdoor pursuits in southern Africa.

BEST BACK-IN-TIME ENTERTAINMENTS

EXPERIENCE TIME TRAVEL WHILE ENJOYING PRESERVED PLEASURES THAT TRANSPORT YOU BACK DECADES, OR EVEN CENTURIES.

01 CIRQUE ROMANÈS, PARIS, FRANCE

This is a unique, magical experience: a red-tented Roma circus in the French capital surrounded by housing blocks. The whole event is mesmerising, with a lost-in-time atmosphere. There are no spangles and sequins here, just circus skills that have been honed in the wasteland around the caravans – from fire-eating to tightrope walking, acrobats to jugglers. The women swish and dance in their long skirts, and the soundtrack is frenetic Balkan folk from the live band.

For more information and tickets see www. cirqueromanes.com; tickets €20 (US$25).

02 FAIRMONT PEACE HOTEL, BUND, SHANGHAI, CHINA

A Shanghai landmark, the tall, graceful Peace Hotel, overlooking the Bund, is one of the most resonant relics of old Shanghai. Its time-capsule nature is even more pronounced as it faces the futurist landscape of Pudong on the opposite riverbank. Renovations have given the hotel's Art Deco interiors a facelift, but one thing remains eternal: the Jazz Bar in the basement. You'll feel transported back to the 1920s and '30s listening to the Old Jazz Band's six veteran musicians (average age: 77).

To book or find out more, visit www. fairmont.com/PeaceHotel; the band plays nightly from 7pm.

03 BALINESE DANCE, INDONESIA

Resembling ancient temple reliefs come to life, Balinese dancers are exquisite, even otherworldly looking, elaborately dressed in outfits of bright colours shot through with delicate gold, with fresh flowers adorning their headdresses. They use stylised hand and feet gestures, as well as eye movements, imbued with ancient meaning. Traditional dances are tied up with religious expression, and tell the stories of the great Hindu epics. But beyond its liturgical function, Balinese dance is also a majestic spectacle, and one that connects you directly to the past.

At Ubud Palace, Jl Raya Ubud, Bali, there are near-nightly performances in a royal setting, while Pura Dalem Ubud, Jl Raya Ubud, is one of the prettiest venues.

⊙ ROYAL OPERA HOUSE TEA DANCE, LONDON, ENGLAND

Harking back to the days when the Royal Opera House was *the* place in London to dance the cha-cha or quick step, it now holds regular tea dances throughout the season in the stately Paul Hamlyn Hall. Huge windows overlook Covent Garden piazza, while the nimble feet of all ages do the steps, and it's all to the accompaniment of the Royal Opera House Dance Band. Sundays here will

transport you to a seemingly gentler time, when dancing meant gliding around a room rather than throwing shapes.

For dates and to buy tickets see the Royal Opera House website at www.roh.org.uk; tickets £10 (US$16).

⊙ GREEK TRAGEDY, AMPHITHEATRE, EPIDAURUS, GREECE

To experience theatre as people did in Ancient Greece, go to the amphitheatre of Epidaurus, one of the world's great buildings, a fan-shaped, open-air auditorium set into a hillside. The amphitheatre is famed for its incredible acoustics – even if an actor speaks quietly, they will be heard from every seat. The theatre is situated within the archaeological site of the Sanctuary of Asklepios, around two hours' drive from Athens. During the annual summer Athens & Epidaurus Festival there are regular performances of ancient classics, such as plays by Euripides. Attend for an uncanny sense of what the experience was like for theatregoers around 2000 years ago. For more details see www.greekfestival. gr/en; most performances take place in August and September; book tickets on +30 210-32 72 000.

✪ QAWAALI SINGERS, DELHI, INDIA

Rather than providing pure entertainment, the Qawaali singers at the shrine of Hazrat Nizamuddin perform for an important religious, devotional purpose. However, the songs after evening prayers are open to all, and visiting when the performance is taking place is a mystical and evocative experience that should not be missed if you're in the area. The devotional concert feels as if it has barely changed for hundreds of years; pilgrims collect smouldering incense and buy trinkets to leave at the shrine, and the hypnotic music mesmerises the crowd. The singing takes place nightly from around sunset at Hazrat Nisamuddin Dargah, Delhi; it's most spectacular on Thursdays and feast days.

✪ SHAKESPEARE'S GLOBE THEATRE, LONDON, ENGLAND

Close to the site of the iconic Elizabethan Globe theatre, London's contemporary Globe was created to evoke the original; a half-timbered theatre-in-the-round, open to the sky. Attending a Shakespeare performance here today is unlike any other theatrical experience, especially if you stand with the 'groundlings', the cheapest price ticket, though you don't have to contend with brawling and lack of toilets as the Elizabethans standing in this area would have. Although you have to stand, there's no better way to feel involved in the show and close to the action. To read more, see the program and book tickets, see www.shakespearesglobe.com; groundling tickets £5 (US$8).

✪ WHIRLING DERVISHES, ISTANBUL, TURKEY

At the Silivrikapı Mevlana Cultural Center you can see the ancient spiritual Sema Ceremony, where whirling dervishes spin to encourage communication with Allah and intoxicate the soul, as has been the tradition for hundreds of years. Of course, this is not entertainment but an important religious ceremony, but it's a beautiful event to experience purely aesthetically as well as spiritually. The dervishes spin with complete control, their long robes circling outwards, forming a pattern like stylised blooms. For information on the regular evening Sema ceremonies, see www.emav.org.

✪ PRESEPE VIVANTI (LIVING NATIVITY), SUTRI, LAZIO, ITALY

Living Nativities – re-enactments of the story of Jesus Christ's birth in a stable – take place all over Italy during Christmas. Some are impressive pageants, some small

TREAD THE BOARDS AT
SHAKESPEARE'S GLOBE
THEATRE, LONDON

and local re-creations of the Christmas story. The one at Sutri in Lazio, a short trip from Rome, is of the latter variety, but deserves particular mention because of its mesmerising, back-in-time setting; the hollowed-out Etruscan tombs that surround the town. The scenes are candlelit; the atmosphere compelling. It definitely feels not-of-this-century.

For more information, contact the Sutri Turismo; check the local town hall website at www.comune.sutri.vt.it, in Italian.

✪ EL MISTERI D'ELX, SPAIN

The Mystery of Elche is one of the world's great mystery plays, depicting the Virgin Mary's death and ascendance into heaven, and is performed every year in the picturesque town of Elche, close to Alicante. The mystical rendering of the story has been performed in this way, in Elche's Basilica of Santa Maria and the evocative Moorish streets of its palm-shaded old town, since the 15th century. To watch is to be suspended in time: it's medieval to its core, with its epic pomp, flowing robes and solemn, emotive processions. The event is on Unesco's List of the Intangible Cultural Heritage of Humanity, and was designated a 'national monument' in 1931.

For more information on the event, which takes place annually over two days in mid-August, see the Elche Tourist Board website at www.visitelche.com.

THE UNLUCKIEST PLACES IN THE WORLD

THE MAYANS THOUGHT THE WORLD WAS GOING TO END IN 2012, BUT COULD '13 BE OUR UNLUCKY YEAR? IF YOU'RE NOT SUPERSTITIOUS, A TRIP TO THESE CURSED DESTINATIONS MIGHT CHANGE YOUR MIND.

01 MAURITIUS

Today Mauritius may be known as an island idyll, but it wasn't always a paradigm of paradise, especially for the dodo. The flightless creature ruled the roost until the Dutch set up shop in the 1600s. Sailors' logs indicate that the dodo wasn't particularly tasty, but the colonists' menagerie of pigs and macaques quickly annihilated the entire species by gorging on their eggs. And it wasn't just this unfortunate bird that vanished after the arrival of Europeans; the red rail, the solitaire and two kinds of sea turtles went the way of the dodo as well, so to speak. Flights fly direct to Mauritius from London, Paris and Johannesburg; www.horizon.mu creates tailor-made vacations.

02 DRAKE PASSAGE, PATAGONIA, CHILE & ARGENTINA

A grey expanse of crashing and curling waves, the Drake Passage cuts between the southern tip of South America and the icy fingers of Antarctica, providing a turbulent route between seas. With winds that gush through at torrential speeds and then suddenly change direction, the passage – named after British explorer Sir Francis Drake – has long been one of the most difficult bodies of water to negotiate; in fact, it's been the demise of countless vessels, including the *San Telmo*, the flagship of the Spanish armada bound for Peru. More than 600 souls were lost.

Cruseros Australis (www.australis.com) is currently the only operator that runs vessels to Cape Horn – the southernmost point in South America.

03 BHANGARH, RAJASTHAN, INDIA

It is believed that in the early 17th century, Madho Singh, a fierce local ruler, sought to construct his capital at Bhangarh. While surveying the land, he met a curious ascetic named Baba Balanath who was engaged in intense thought. The devotee allowed the ruler to build his fortress but warned him that the shadow of his palace could not pass over his cherished meditation spot.

Madho Singh obliged, but years later Ajab Singh – his arrogant progeny – added on to the sprawling fort, unleashing a string of uncanny events that swiftly led to the city's undoing. Today, it's a ghost town.

Base yourself in Jaipur, 75km away, and live like a king at the ITC Rajputana; www. itchotels.in/hotels/itcrajputana.aspx.

✪ TOWER OF LONDON, LONDON, ENGLAND

The infamous Tower of London is where many unlucky nobles met their untimely end at the edge of the executioner's blade. Popular spirits said to walk the brick and stone halls include Thomas Beckett and Henry VI. Perhaps the most chilling tale is that of the Countess of Salisbury, who in 1541 – after being charged with criminal wrongdoings – tried a running escape from the gallows, but was swiftly captured and hacked to pieces by her masked executioner. Some people claim to have seen her grisly death acted out by the resident spirits.

The Tower of London (www.hrp.org.uk/toweroflondon) is open 9am to 5.30pm Tuesday to Saturday, and 10am to 5.30pm Sunday and Monday. Tickets are £18 (US$28) when purchased online.

✪ BERMUDA TRIANGLE, ATLANTIC OCEAN

No unlucky list would be complete without the famed isosceles of doom that spreads across the Atlantic Ocean from the shores of Florida, over to San Juan,

TAKING ON DRAKE PASSAGE IN ANTARCTICA

Puerto Rico, and up to the pink-tinged sands of its namesake, Bermuda. The idea of the ominous Bermuda Triangle grew in popularity during the 1950s when five fighter planes mysteriously disappeared during a training mission. It has since secured its place in modern legend after subsequent tragedies befell additional planes and boats. Sceptics blame magnetic fields and hurricane-prone winds; kookier theorists believe that the work of extra-terrestrials may be to blame.

The main airports near the Bermuda triangle, should you not wish to arrive by ship, are Miami International (www.miami-airport.com) and Nassau in the Bahamas (www.nas.bs).

✪ UNLUCKY LAKE, SASKATCHEWAN, CANADA

Canada has long been known for its quirky place names, such as Medicine Hat or Moose Factory, which have their roots in aboriginal lore, but the moniker of this prairie puddle – in the middle of Saskatchewan's lakes – is a mystery. Perhaps there was a fruitless fishing season many years ago? Besides the hard beds at the nearby motel, there doesn't seem to be anything particularly unlucky about this place besides its name...

Unlucky Lake is within in the confines of Meadow Lake Provincial Park (www.saskparks.net/MeadowLake), roughly 4½ hours north of Saskatoon.

☯ TUTANKHAMUN'S TOMB, VALLEY OF THE KINGS, EGYPT

Nothing's unluckier than a good curse, and no one knew how to better conjure up a wicked spell than the ancient Egyptian pharaohs. Though difficult to completely decipher, the markings on Tutankhamun's crypt were thought to be warnings against looters and marauders – threats that were ignored by Howard Carter and his team of archaeologists when they cracked open the tomb, effectively launching the modern era of Egyptology. Six weeks later, Lord Carnarvon – the group's benefactor – died from an infected mosquito bite, and by the end of the year six more members of the group had perished from unexplained fevers and murders.

When in Luxor, try Salahadeen (095 236 5081), which offers a set menu of Egyptian home-style favourites. Go local and dip your breads in the tasty sauces.

☯ ROSE HALL, MONTEGO BAY, JAMAICA

When it comes to curses, nothing quite beats a good voodoo spell, and Annie Palmer really knew how to spread her fair share of disease, despair and death. It is commonly believed that Annie – the one-time proprietor of Rose Hall – was responsible for the murder of three husbands and many lovers during the course of a decade, until she herself was killed as she slept. Today, she regularly wanders around her house with a coterie of murdered men, stalking visitors and causing bloodstains to appear as if from thin air.

Half Moon (halfmoon.rockresorts.com), a 160-hectare luxury resort, is the ultimate Caribbean getaway.

☯ INOKASHIRA PARK, TOKYO, JAPAN

With dozens of spooky locales depicted in Japanese horror films, it might come as a surprise that one of the unluckiest places in Tokyo is the peaceful Inokashira Park, located on the city's western edge and hemmed by delicate cherry blossoms in the spring. Locals believe that if a couple takes a rowboat out onto the lake their relationship is destined to end. This is largely attributed to the fact that the deity Benzaiten is worshipped at a shrine nearby, and she is commonly believed to ignite jealousy and distrust among loved ones. Pair a visit to Inokashira Park with a stop at the Ghibli Museum (www.ghibli-museum. jp/en/), home to Hayao Miyazaki's oeuvre. Ticket must be booked in advance.

☯ HYANNIS PORT, MASSACHUSETTS, USA

Known for their combed coiffures and 'pahk the cah' Boston drawls, the Kennedys have long been considered American royalty, and their unofficial headquarters is a large seaside estate in Cape Cod's Hyannis Port known as the Kennedy Compound. Although they have enjoyed the trappings of a veritable aristocracy, the family has seen their share of unlucky incidents during the past few decades – namely from 1940 to 2000. From multiple plane crashes to devastating assassinations, the 'Kennedy Curse' may be a fabrication of the media, but it remains rather uncanny just how many unlucky events can befall one household.

Dine nearby at the Barnstable Restaurant and Tavern (www.barnstablerestaurant.com) in the heart of historic Barnstable Village.

CITIES WITH BIKE-SHARING SCHEMES

KEEP FIT, STAY GREEN, BEAT CONGESTION, LIVE VISCERALLY AND TAKE IN A CITY'S SIGHTS ON TWO WHEELS IN A GROWING NUMBER OF BIKE-SHARING SCHEMES.

01 PARIS, FRANCE

Bicycles give you freedom, or so Paris' Vélib would like you to believe; the name is a contraction of *vélo liberté*, meaning 'freedom bike'. Sitting pretty in a city that hosts cycling's biggest stage race, the Tour de France, 20,600 bikes await potential users in 1450 docking stations spaced a handy 300m apart. Thanks to its ambitious size and heavy usage, Vélib has become a blueprint for bike-sharing schemes worldwide, though it gained early notoriety for its high number of thefts. Pilfered *petite reines* (little queens), as the bikes are known, have been found as far away as North Africa.

The 24-hour access fee is €1.70 (US$2); usage charges for 30min/1hr/2hrs free/€1/7 (US$1.20/9). For more information see www.velib.paris.fr.

02 HANGZHOU, CHINA

If you want to see how far China has embraced green living come to Hangzhou, Zhejiang province's oasis of urban beauty and proud home of the world's second-largest bike-sharing scheme (fellow Chinese city Wuhan is first). Hangzhou's statistics make Paris' Vélib look almost insignificant: 60,000 bikes residing in 2500 docking stations, most of which have been cleverly integrated to link up with the public transportation network. Nearly 250,000 people in this 6.7 million-strong metropolis use the bikes daily, taking advantage of a generous borrowing scheme which offers residents and visitors the first hour of usage for free.

Special Z cards procured at City Smart Card centres can be used to store up to ¥300 (US$47) of usage time.

03 COPENHAGEN, DENMARK

Rivalled only by Amsterdam for its bike friendliness, Copenhagen has a long history of sustainable transportation. Today, 37% of daily commutes in the Danish capital are undertaken by bicycle and its bike-sharing scheme, introduced in 1995, was the first of the modern city

models. Copenhagen's system is unique in that the borrowing is free; you just push a 20 kroner returnable coin into a slot to release your bike like a shopping trolley. The bikes, which are currently being upgraded, are famously durable. In 2005, in a publicity stunt, a Danish journalist rode one 3500km from Copenhagen to Istanbul inside a month.

Access deposit is DKK20 (US$3); usage is free. Bikes are available March–November. For more information: www.bycyklen.dk.

two-wheeled machines were a surprising hit; usage during the first year was an average 25,000 per day and it has been rumoured that even members of the royal family ride them. Edging east from London's 'square mile' financial district, Boris bikes' geographical reach will be extended in 2012 to the borders of the summer Olympics site. The 24-hour access fee is £1 (US$1.50); usage charges for 30min/1hr/2hrs free/£1/6 (US$1.50/9). For more information see www.tfl.gov.uk.

✪ LONDON, ENGLAND

London's 6000 'Boris bikes', named after city mayor and avid cyclist Boris Johnson, first graced the UK capital's asphalt in July 2010 in a scheme based on Montreal's Bixi. On streets more accustomed to red double-decker buses and black taxis, the 23kg

✪ MONTREAL, CANADA

Montrealers are a hardy bunch to whom the odd October snow flurry *n'est pas un problème*. Nevertheless, cycling in a city where January temperatures can plummet to -20°C requires a bit of seasonal adjustment. Consequently, Montreal's Bixi

scheme – the first comprehensive bike-share in Canada – hibernates in November and reopens in April when the weather is less frigid. Using aluminium, puncture-resistant bikes and smart solar-powered technology to fire its 405 docking stations, Bixi's 2009 launch was so successful that the company has gone on to found bike schemes in numerous other cities including London, Washington DC and Toronto. The 24-hour access fee is C$5 (US$5); usage charges for 30min/1hr/2hrs free/C$1.50/10.50 (US$1.50/10.50). For more information see montreal.bixi.com.

✪ TEL AVIV, ISRAEL
Bike-sharing arrived in the Middle East in May 2011 with the inauguration of Tel Aviv's Tel-o-fun system stocked with 1500 green bikes, most of which come handily equipped with adaptable child-seats pinned over the back wheel. In a country well known for its collective kibbutz spirit, the sharing system has been well received by urban communities whose apartment-style living leaves little room for bike storage. More than 70km of marked bike lanes, many of them traversing the city's attractive beachfront, add a touch of class to the cycling infrastructure. The 24-hour access fee is 14NIS (US$3.50); usage charge for 30min/1hr/2½hrs free/3NIS/30 (US$0.80/8). For more information see www.tel-o-fun.co.il.

✪ WASHINGTON DC, USA
Bixi rides again in the US capital! The nation's second big-city bike-sharing

scheme, founded in 2010 and known locally as CaBi (Capital Bikeshare), is funded by public money and largely apes the road-tested system set up in Montreal a year earlier. Although relatively small by European or Chinese standards, Washington's average usage of 4000 daily trips is an encouraging start in a country that has long had a love-in with the motor car. What's more, technology geeks equipped with a smartphone can download a free app called Spotcycle which informs you of bicycle availability at the nearest docking station.

The 24-hour access fee is US$7; usage charges for 30min/1hr/2hrs free/US$2/14. For more information see www.capitalbikeshare.com.

❂ MELBOURNE, AUSTRALIA

Melbourne Bike Share, introduced in 2010, was slow out of the blocks in such an ostensibly sports-loving city thanks primarily to its helmet law. The Australian city's scheme was the first in the world to insist on mandatory helmets and early figures (only 250 users a day) suggested reluctance to adapt to the rule. Undeterred, city authorities have begun offering cheap helmets from strategically located vending machines and numbers have picked up. Another Melbourne quirk is its bike-share tours, designed to orientate visitors to the intricacies of the sharing system and the sights of the city.

The 24-hour access fee is A$2.60 (US$2.50); usage charge for 30min/1hr/2hrs free/A$2/17 (US$2/16). For more information see www.melbournebikeshare.com.au.

❂ MEXICO CITY, MEXICO

The planet's most improbable and possibly most necessary bike scheme (given the pollution) kicked off in February 2010 with the city authorities rescinding a mandatory helmet law to encourage more subscribers. The system, Ecobici, was an immediate success, garnering 30,000 subscribers in its first year and expanding its coverage beyond Mexico City's Federal District into the historical core. There are 1000 bikes, with each being utilised on average eight times per day, but unlike other schemes, Ecobici is for residents only who pay annual subscriptions. Not surprisingly, in a city of 21 million, there's a long waiting list.

Annual subscription is M$300 (US$22); usage charges for 45min/1hr/2hrs free/M$10/45 (US$0.70/3). For more information see www.ecobici.df.gob.mx.

❂ SEVILLE, SPAIN

Few cities have undergone such radical greening in recent years as Seville which, since 2007, has initiated an underground metro, a tram system and a pioneering bike-share scheme, Sevici. Turning your pedals in Andalucia's flat, balmy cultural capital while inhaling the aroma of ripening oranges is one of Spain's most enjoyable outdoor experiences, made easier by the city's traffic-light arterial roads, many of which have been pedestrianised to accommodate trams and bikes. Sevici offers a minimum of seven days access to short-term visitors – a good incentive to extend your stay!

Seven-day access fee is €10 (US$13); usage charges for 30min/1hr/2hrs free/€1/3 (US$1.20/4). More information see www.sevici.es, in Spanish.

BEST PLACES TO SEE ELEPHANTS (UP CLOSE)

THERE'S NOTHING QUITE LIKE AN ELEPHANT ENCOUNTER TO GAIN SOME PERSPECTIVE ON LIFE (AND WE'RE NOT TALKING ZOOS). HERE ARE OUR TOP PICKS.

01 CHOBE NATIONAL PARK & OKAVANGO DELTA, BOTSWANA

With an elephant population of 70,000, the highest concentration in the world, Chobe tops the bucket list of any ellie lover. This is a pachyderm paradise: you'll hear the calls and rumbles of these Kalahari kings, the largest of all elephants, see them in massive groups at the river (don't get *too* close), and encounter them on the road. Got an elephantine bank balance? Venture outside the park to the sumptuous Abu camp for one-on-one time with the on-site herd, and take up the rare opportunity to snooze among the elephants in the 'star bed' overlooking their *boma* (enclosure). During the dry season the ellies congregate around the Chobe and Linyanti river in Chobe; in the rainy season head for the southeast of the national park.

02 HONGSA, LAOS

Situated on an emerald plain ringed by densely forested mountains, the remote town of Hongsa, Sayaboury province, is little-touched by modern life. For Laos, once called the 'land of a million elephants', it's elephant central: with a concentration of domesticated elephants in this part of the province, mahouts still carry on an age-old tradition with their charges, working in the logging industry. Give an ellie and its owner a well-deserved day away from the grind by inviting them to be your tour guides. There are also elephant encounters of hefty proportions in mid-February at the Elephant Festival in Sayaboury, a day devoted to all things elephant.

Hongsa is a day's journey by public bus from Luang Prabang. For accommodation try the Jumbo Guesthouse at www. lotuselephant.com.

03 SELOUS RESERVE, TANZANIA

You've heard of peeping toms, but how about an elephant trunk peeking over the top of your bathroom door? Or being escorted to your tent by an ellie (and a Maasai guard) after breakfasting mere steps

EXPLORE BOTSWANA'S OKAVANGO DELTA BY CANOE OR ELEPHANT

from the massive and beautiful creature? More rustic and untamed than many areas on the safari circuit, the Lake Manze area in southern Tanzania is a prime site for daily elephant encounters as they amble through camps on their way to water points. Gliding along the river on a boat safari, don't be surprised if you're obliged to stop several minutes for an elephant crossing.

The Selous Reserve is an approximately 40-minute flight from Dar es Salaam. Stay at www.lakemanze.com.

✪ MARGATE CITY, USA

Stuck on North American soil and don't like zoos? Get a different kind of elephant high by visiting Lucy the Elephant: the first ever, patented 'zoomorphic' building, constructed of wood and tin in the 1880s. Fashioned in the image of the world's most beloved creature, all 20m and six storeys of Lucy are still standing tall — the howdah carriage atop her back was once a lookout point — and she's listed on the national historical register. While Lucy can be spotted from miles away, you can't get much closer to an elephant than this: her interior has faithfully served as a real-estate office, summer cottage and tavern.

Lucy is located at 9200 Atlantic Ave, Margate City, 15 minutes from Atlantic City. See www.lucytheelephant.org.

❂ SOUTHERN DAMARALAND, NAMIBIA

No, you're not hallucinating. In the piercingly bright light and rolling sandscapes of western Namibia stands before you a genuine herd of ellies, though they may look a bit otherworldly. They represent a unique species and only one of two populations of desert elephants in the world (the other's in Mali). Conservation efforts have helped the population increase considerably this century but they're often scattered far and wide in the search for water. Get acquainted with the desert ellies by a team of elephant trackers who document the herds, monitor their movements, camp under the stars and help elephants and humans cohabitate. Learn more at www.desertelephant.org.

❂ TSAVO NATIONAL PARK EAST, KENYA

If you've never seen a red elephant – aside from that stuffed animal in your nephew's play box – head straight to East Tsavo for some famously unique-looking ellies. They weren't born that way, but you'll soon learn elephants love to roll and play in the dust, and this is an area where there's plenty: a few rolls around and they're coated in a rusty hue. The population of elephants in Kenya is 36,000 and about a third of them live in the Tsavo-Mkomazi ecosystem, so chances are you'll see a bunch.

Check with the Kenyan Wildlife Service for up-to-date information on campsites: www.kws.org or book direct at the Voi Safari Lodge.

PUCKER UP IN CHIANG MAI, THAILAND

UDAWALAWE NATIONAL PARK, SRI LANKA

Happily munching on a vegetarian buffet and trampling through the marshes and open grasslands, an estimated 250 or more Sri Lankan elephants – the most speckled of the subspecies, and darker – permanently live on the Udawalawe reserve. See young ellies at the Elephant Transit Centre, an orphanage where they can be protected and nurtured through their early years. You can't exactly hold their bottles, but observing a collection of young calves (39 at last count) at close range while they feed is a sight to behold. Human contact is minimised so that one day these tots can live on the wild side. Accommodation can be reserved through the national park or try www. kalushideaway.com.

MFUWE LODGE, SOUTH LUANGWE NATIONAL PARK, ZAMBIA

You're not the only one who loves those succulent sweet mangoes: the ellies love them, too! One herd is so partial to a particular wild mango tree, they showed up one day at the newly constructed lobby of the Mfuwe Lodge in Zambia and proceeded to traipse through just to get to their fix. The parade of pachyderms made international news and the mango migration carries on: the 10-strong herd arrives each year when the luscious fruit ripens. Guests can see them up-close at Mfuwe's base camp. The elephants make their yearly pilgrimage to the mango tree for four to six weeks between October and December. See www. mfuwelodge.com.

MONDULKIRI, CAMBODIA

The dense forest crackles under your feet, an eagle swoops and you're serenaded by the sounds of gibbons as you spend time with the ellies in northern Cambodia's province of Mondulkiri, home of the Bunong tribe and about half of the country's ageing domestic elephant population. A handful of them are now getting R&R at the Elephant Valley Project, a sanctuary that encourages the mahouts to retire their charges and tend to them on this sustainable forest reserve. You can feed them bananas, muck about with the gentle giants as they take their baths or simply sit and watch them close-up. Guest accommodation is available in bungalows or dorm-style in hammocks. The project is located 11km from Sen Morom, an area known for its waterfalls and trekking. See www.elephantvalleyproject.com.

CHIANG MAI, THAILAND

Throughout Asia the centuries-old tradition of domesticating and tending to elephants created a lifelong career for people known as mahouts – who would train and work one-on-one with an elephant for decades, creating a unique bond. Get a chance to be a mahout for a day (or more) and be paired with an elephant while you learn basic commands to communicate, get to scrub them down, and even have a chance for a short ride behind those elephant ears. For more information, see www. baanchangelephantpark.com or the Elephant Nature Park near Chiang Mai, see www.elephantnaturepark.org.

BEST PLACES TO DO
SOMETHING NEW

IT'S HUMAN NATURE TO WANT TO BE THE FIRST. THESE ACTIVITIES ARE NOT JUST NEW TO YOU, THEY'RE NEW TO THE WORLD. SO BE THE AMONG THE FIRST TO GET YOUR BRAGGING RIGHTS.

 o1 WATCH THE NEWEST SPORT: PHILADELPHIA, USA

Make haste to Philadelphia, Pennsylvania to 'join the revolution' – that's the official slogan of kronum, the world's newest sport. A mashup of football, basketball and rugby (with a dash of quidditch for good measure), it's played on a special one-of-a-kind circular field – hence the trip to Philly. Billed as 'fast-paced, action-packed and unpredictable', it was invented in 2008 and aims to be the first major sport invented in a century. We're not sure whether it'll rival baseball or football for sports fans' hearts – there are currently only six teams in the US-only Kronum League – but it's certainly fun to watch.

Get more info and game dates at www.kronum.com.

----

o2 SEE THE NEWEST ANIMAL: THE PHILIPPINES

What's two metres long, lives in the trees and has a double penis? *Varanus bitatawa*, of course. The enormous monitor lizard, though well-known to local tribes (who consider it tasty eatin'), was only identified by scientists in 2009. A

herbivorous relative of the komodo dragon, it's about as close to a dinosaur as you're going to get. To spot one, head to the misty Sierra Madre mountains on the Philippines island of Luzon and cross your fingers – the secretive tree-dwelling lizards only spend about 20 minutes a day on the ground.

Arrange a guided trek of Northern Sierra Madre Natural park by visiting the mayor's office in the town of San Mariano.

---

03 EXPLORE THE NEWEST FRONTIER: OUTER SPACE

All of a sudden, the future is here. Space travel, once a kiddie fantasy ('I'm gonna be an astronaut when I grow up!') is suddenly a reality for ordinary citizens (at least, those who can afford it). In 2012 several private companies will blast off, carrying tourists into the great blackness of outer space. For $200,000, you can book a seat on Virgin Galactic's 2½-hour suborbital flight, which includes a six-minute interval of weightlessness. Virgin trips take off from the newly built Spaceport America in Las Cruces, New Mexico, where passengers spend three days training before liftoff.

If you've got a couple of hundred grand to spare to fulfil your astronaut fantasies, see www.virgingalactic.com.

✪ TRY THE NEWEST JUNK FOOD: US STATE FAIRS

In terms of sheer novelty, America's annual state fairs beat chic palaces of molecular gastronomy by a country mile. Each year, fairs compete to come up with the most bizarre, artery-clogging invention. In 2011 California's San Diego County Fair came up with deep-fried Kool-Aid – a creation consisting of battered and oil-dunked Kool-Aid brand fruit drink. Not to be beaten, North Carolina countered with deep-fried bubble gum. Iowa fought back with deep-fried butter on a stick, while Texas honoured its Tex-Mex roots with deep-fried salsa. You may call it disgusting; we call it pure, unadulterated Americana.

Most state fairs take place in the summer or autumn (fall).

✪ VISIT THE NEWEST COUNTRY: SINT MAARTEN

OK, technically the world's newest country is South Sudan. But barring active war zones, the newest country is the Caribbean's Sint Maarten. Until 2010 it was a territory of the Netherland Antilles. Now, it's a constituent country of the Netherlands. Of course this doesn't actually change much on the ground. But in Sint Maarten, nothing needed to change – when you've got pink-sand beaches, sparkling cerulean seas and charming colonial towns, why mess with perfection? So grab a piña colada and head straight for the warm waters of Simpson Bay.

The official website www.st-maarten.com has tons of local travel information.

✪ TREK THE NEWEST HIKING TRAIL: ISRAEL

Starting in Nazareth and winding through hills and olive groves to the ancient town of Capernaum, the 63km Gospel Trail supposedly follows the footsteps of Jesus. Opened in late 2011, the trail intends to attract Christian tourists interested in exploring the area. But you don't need to be religious to enjoy the trail, which passes through the verdant Jezreel Valley, the shaded Beit Qeshet Oak Reserve and the arid slopes of Mt Arbel before ending at the shimmering Sea of Galilee.

Israel's Ministry of Tourism site, www.goisrael.com, has much more info on the trail and stops along the way.

✪ VISIT THE NEWEST CITY: SONGDO, SOUTH KOREA

Like something out of a sci-fi film, the world's newest city is rising, full-fledged, from the South Korean flatlands 65km west of Seoul. Songdo, a master-planned

city, aims to avoid the plagues of many Asian megalopolises – pollution, overcrowding, gridlocked traffic – through careful design and environmentally sustainable building standards. Like Las Vegas, Songdo will replicate international landmarks such as the Venice canals and New York's Central Park, while also building its own signature buildings such as the planned 151-floor Incheon Tower. While the city won't be entirely finished until 2015, the Sheraton Hotel is already open for curious guests.

See www.songdo.com for interactive maps and other information.

✪ SEE THE NEWEST ISLAND: ZUBAIR ISLANDS, YEMEN

Following volcanic eruptions in late 2011, the world's newest island was born in a part of the Red Sea belonging to Yemen. Part of an island group known as the Zubair Islands, the unnamed protrusion of volcanic rock is a rarity – most volcanic islands crumble back into the sea shortly after their creation. Though Yemen's political instability is currently making travel there a difficult undertaking, the Zubair Islands are said to have magnificent scuba diving around their underwater volcanic outcroppings. We're sure this baby island will be no different.

Check out www.yementourism.com for info on diving the Zubair Islands.

✪ TRY THE NEWEST FOOD TREND: COPENHAGEN, DENMARK

Crowned the World's Best Restaurant in 2011, Copenhagen's Noma has been

ESCALOPES FLAVOURED WITH
LEEK FLOWERS BY RENÉ REDZEPI
AT NOMA, COPENHAGEN

instrumental in introducing a radical new concept in dining: foraged cuisine. Chef René Redzepi has achieved rock-star status for his gathering skills, combing the countryside for local lichens, mosses, pine needles and other things generally not recognised as food. Critics have been raving over his earthy cuisine, and other chefs are taking note: the foraging trend has spread far and wide – ingredients such as wild sorrel, yarrow and acorns are popping up on menus from Los Angeles to London. If you want to try Noma, better get a head start: the restaurant books up months and months in advance.
For more information see www.noma.dk.

○ EXPERIENCE THE NEWEST VACATION CONCEPT: ST VINCENT AND THE GRENADINES

From 2012, the Caribbean islands of St Vincent and the Grenadines are offering the 'digital detox' vacation. Guests arriving in the islands hand over their smartphones, laptops and other devices, and receive personal coaching about living the unplugged life. Participating hotels help guests keep their resolution by removing TVs and other electronics from the rooms. Fortunately, the island offers plenty of low-tech distractions, from snorkelling to jungle hikes to sailing the azure seas.
See www.discoversvg.com for more.

THE BEST CAPITAL CITIES BUILT FROM SCRATCH

WHY STICK WITH THE SAME OLD BORING CAPITAL CITIES WHEN YOU COULD BUILD A NEW ONE FROM SCRATCH? WE RUN THROUGH PURPOSE-BUILT CAPITALS AROUND THE WORLD...

01 ASTANA, KAZAKHSTAN, 1997

A lonely outpost ravaged by bitterly cold winds, the provincial town of Akmola wasn't the bookies' favourite to be named capital of the newly independent Kazakhstan in 1994. Nonetheless, the menace of earthquakes and a general lack of building space meant the original capital Almaty lost its crown, and the president et al packed their bags for its smaller successor in the steppe. Akmola was duly renamed 'Astana' (an imaginative feat of rebranding that means 'Capital') and has slowly transformed into a *Blade Runner*-esque metropolis in the middle of nowhere, with no shortage of space-age monuments. Take the lift to the top of the lollipop-shaped Bayterek monument (locals affectionately call it Chupa Chups); it's open from 10am to 10pm.

02 BRASÍLIA, BRAZIL, 1960

The idea of building a capital closer to the centre of Brazil was first dreamt up in the early 19th century, but it was more than a century later when construction began on Brasília. The town quickly became a test lab for modernist architecture – artificial lakes, sprawling parks and wide highways were designed to make for a leafy, utopian metropolis (along with a few flying saucer-shaped buildings thrown in for good measure). Some grumble it's all looking a bit tired 50 years on – others cheerfully point to the fact that it looks like a giant aeroplane when seen from above.

The Santuário Dom Bosco is an architectural highlight of Brasília – a modern church illuminated by tinted-blue glass; it's open from 7am to 7pm.

03 WASHINGTON DC, USA, 1790

Though it may be older than most planned capitals, Washington DC's glorious existence started in the same way as many others – as a compromise arrangement. Given its own special, stateless wedge of land – today known as the District of Columbia – the city was meant to be independent from bickering factions of

IWO JIMA MEMORIAL WITH
WASHINGTON MONUMENT AND
CAPITOL BUILDING BEHIND

northern and southern states, with its site handpicked by President George Washington himself. Ever since, the city's fortunes have mirrored those of the United States – attacked by the British in the 19th century and by Al Qaeda in the 21st, its streets have also been the battleground of the Civil Rights movement and anti-Vietnam war demonstrations.

Washington's Capitol is the point around which the city was planned. The visitor centre offers guided tours of the building – see www.visitthecapitol.gov.

✪ ABUJA, NIGERIA, 1991

With Nigeria's ethnic and religious tensions threatening to tear the country apart, Abuja was chosen as a neutral middle ground at the centre of the country – replacing the overpopulated leviathan city of Lagos on the southern coast. Twenty years on, Abuja is still playing catch-up with its predecessor – it has less than a tenth of Lagos' population, and a fraction of its commercial clout. Fortunately it has compensated by building a number of grandiose structures – but none are as impressive as Aso Rock, the craggy cliffs that preside smugly over the city.

Wuse market is Abuja's favourite place to go shopping, stocking everything from boxer shorts to bananas. It's busy most of the week – come prepared to haggle.

✪ NAY PYI TAW, MYANMAR, 2005

Myanmar's new capital city popped up under peculiar circumstances a few years ago in a remote corner of the country, and has remained something of a mystery ever since. A bizarre town of six-lane motorways, King Kong–sized statues and grandiose palaces, it was built under the stewardship of Myanmar's military dictators – allegedly on the advice of general Than Shwe's personal astrologer. It's been little visited by outsiders since – those who are able to travel there mostly remark on the enormous scale of the place, and its eerily empty streets.

The National Herbal Park counts as one of Nay Pyi Taw's very few tourist attractions – last we heard, entry is free.

✪ ISLAMABAD, PAKISTAN, 1967

Built as a capital to crown the newly independent Pakistan, Islamabad took the reins after the powers that be decided that the old capital, Karachi, was vulnerable to attacks from the sea. Fifty years on, and Islamabad's tourism industry teeters somewhere between small and nonexistent but urban development has carried on undeterred. Dominating the skyline is the Shah Faisal Mosque – a gift from Saudi Arabia designed in the style of a Bedouin tent. A dubious urban legend has it that the CIA suspected its minarets were missiles. The Shah Faisal Mosque is located at the north of the city, at the foot of the Margalla Hills. Non-Muslims are welcome, but are asked not to visit during prayer times.

✪ CANBERRA, AUSTRALIA, 1913

With Melbourne and Sydney scrapping over the title of Australian capital, it was decided that the lowly settlement of

Canberra would get top honours instead. Work started on the city in 1913 – although unimpressed Aussies initially dubbed it 'six suburbs in search of a city' and 'a cemetery with lights'. Various additions and tweaks followed in the years thereafter, and today Canberra has a sedate charm of its own, with national institutions and museums arranged around Lake Burley Griffin – an artificial body of water dug up in the 1960s. Visit the National Carillon on the edge of the lake – a musical tower that chimes out melodies at lunchtimes on Mondays, Wednesdays, Fridays and Sundays.

✪ NEW DELHI, INDIA, 1911

New Delhi simultaneously manages to be both a new capital city and a very old one. By the time the British Empire was getting itchy feet in its capital at Kolkata, Delhi was already an old hand – it had been the site of seven successive ancient cities and had at various points already ruled over whole swathes of the Indian subcontinent. This didn't stop the British from going one further and building 'New' Delhi – a spacious city of bungalows and boulevards built up around the ancient sites – that is still the Indian capital today.

Don't leave without visiting the National Museum of India – a whistle-stop tour through 5000 years of Indian history. It's open Tuesday to Sunday.

✪ BELMOPAN, BELIZE, 1970

With Belize City completely wrecked by Hurricane Hattie in 1961, the authorities of British Honduras sensibly decided that there was nothing for it but to pack their bags

NEW MEETS OLD IN INDIA'S CAPITAL, DELHI

and shift their capital city inland – a safe distance from the ravages of the Caribbean Sea. Despite being initially met with incredulity by the international community, little Belmopan has clung on against the odds. It gets few visitors – among them Prince Harry, who caused a minor sensation by throwing some dance moves at a street party last year.

Pay a visit to the Belize Archives Department, which has various displays on the country's history – its website is at www.belizearchives.gov.bz.

✪ RAMCIEL, SOUTH SUDAN, 2016?

What's the first thing you do when you find yourself in charge of the world's newest country? Why, set about building the world's newest capital city of course! Such is the thinking behind the South Sudanese government's decision to up sticks from their current capital Juba to the proposed city of Ramciel in their country's central grasslands. The proposed move isn't without its opponents – some think that the money required to build a flashy capital would be best spent elsewhere, particularly given the extremely high levels of poverty in South Sudan.

At the time of writing, Ramciel was little more than a construction site – find out about what's going on at www.ramcielconstruction.com.

MARVELLOUS METEOROLOGICAL SITES

MANY OF US TRAVEL IN SEARCH OF SUNSHINE. BUT THERE'S MUCH MORE TO EXPERIENCE THAN MERE GOLDEN RAYS. SO, EVERYWHERE YOU GO, ALWAYS TAKE A GOOD LOOK AT THE WEATHER WITH YOU.

01 CATATUMBO LIGHTNING, LAKE MARACAIBO, VENEZUELA

Catatumbo National Park comes as something of a shock. Unusual climate conditions – thought to result from the unique proximity of 5000m-high peaks (the Andes) and a sea-level reservoir (Lake Maracaibo) – cause one of the world's longest and most consistent lightning displays, though its power has diminished somewhat in recent years. Even still, on average the skies here are electrified on 160 nights a year, with bolts striking up to 40 times a minute for up to nine hours, visible from 400km away. Strangely, though, the associated thunder is inaudible, rendering this fury an eerily silent spectacle.

Tours to Catatumbo can be arranged from Mérida; lightning is more likely during the wet season (May to December).

02 MOONBOW, VICTORIA FALLS, ZAMBIA/ZIMBABWE

Mosi-oa-Tunya (the Smoke that Thunders) is no ordinary waterfall. Here, a 1700m-wide sheet of Zambezi River plunges more than 100m into the gorge below. And here, on certain evenings, it puts on some extra sparkle. By day, rainbows often arc over this roaring cascade, caused by sunlight reflecting off the considerable spray. But when the moon's full and the sky's cloud-free, the same happens at night – though colours are barely discernible due to the fainter light. Stand on the Zambian side just after moonrise for the best chance of a glimpse. Just watch out for the buffalo and elephant that like night-walking too.

Moonbows are best seen April to July, when water levels are highest, thus creating sufficient spray.

03 MORNING GLORY, GULF OF CARPENTARIA, AUSTRALIA

There's a wonderful Aussie-ness to weather prediction in far-north outback Queensland. They say: if a brisk sea breeze has been blowing through Burketown, and if the fridges in the pub have frosted over, there's a good chance the next day will bring a

Morning Glory. Scientific? Maybe not. But the Gulf of Carpentaria is the only place where these enormous roll clouds – often 1000km long, 1km to 2km high, hovering just 100m above the ground and travelling at up to 60km/hour – can be predictably seen. And scientifically forecast or otherwise, it's worth raising a tinny to that. Morning Glories form early in the day in September and October; scenic flights are available from Burketown.

✪ TORNADO ALLEY, MIDWEST USA

There is no Tornado Alley. At least, not in a discrete, accurately mappable sense. But there is a clump of the American midwest – states such as Oklahoma, Kansas, Texas and the Dakotas – where whirlwinds whip through with particular oomph and frequency: 90% of the USA's tornadoes twist here, as the cold, dry Rocky Mountain air hits the moist breezes from the Gulf of Mexico. Peak time for such Dorothy-bothering cyclones is May to June, when the best plan is to hole up in Oklahoma City or Denver, and be ready to make a dash when you hear the forecast...

Storm Chasing Adventure Tours runs small, six-day trips in Tornado Alley; see www.stormchasing.com.

✪ EXTREME COLD, ANTARCTICA

It's no surprise the planet's coldest temperature was recorded in Antarctica – a downright nippy -89.2°C at the Russian Vostok Station. Much stranger is the fact that the White Continent is a desert, due to its lack of rain. It's scientists who feel the region's

LET'S TWIST AGAIN: TORNADO TRACKERS IN THE MIDWEST, USA

harshest extremes – they visit the coldest, darkest reaches at the coldest, darkest times. Passing travellers get off lighter, most cruising to the wildlife-crazy Antarctic Peninsula in summer, when the weather's a 'balmy' 0°C – the mere tip of the iceberg. Most Antarctic expeditions depart from Ushuaia, Argentina; the summer cruise season runs from November to March.

⊙ CAMANCHACAS, ATACAMA DESERT, CHILE

The Atacama Desert is a mighty parched place. The region sees an annual average of less than 1mm of rain; some areas haven't had so much as drizzle for 400 years. Barren plains are prevalent, soil is Mars-like, ancient bodies are mummified by the arid air. And yet there is life here – largely thanks to the camanchacas, vast banks of marine fog that float inland off the Pacific and provide a few cleverly adapted residents (llama-like guanacos, foxes, prickly cacti) with a little liquid. Sit and watch the mists roll in, and you may also glimpse the wildlife taking a grateful drink. San Pedro de Atacama is the region's tourism hub; it is 1670km and a 20-hour bus ride from Santiago.

⊙ AURORA BOREALIS, ABISKO, SWEDEN

The time is nigh to catch the most magical of celestial spectacles: NASA has predicted 2012–13 will see a 50-year peak in auroral activity. And what activity – the northern lights are the ballerinas of the meteorological world. Graceful shimmers of green, yellow and red, they pirouette and cabriole across the skies, a dazzling dance

on a heavenly stage. The performance can be seen at high latitudes all over the northern hemisphere, but clear and perpetually cloudless Abisko is one of the best spots – during winter at this outpost in Swedish Lapland, the lights come out to play almost every night.
Abisko is 100km west of Kiruna, which has an airport. The best time for aurora viewing is December to March.

⊙ MONSOON, MEGHALAYA, INDIA

In Hindi, Meghalaya means 'Home of the Clouds' – an appropriate epithet for India's soggiest state, wherein lie a couple of contenders for 'world's wettest place'. The village of Mawsynram, tucked into the unsurprisingly lush East Khasi Hills, receives an annual average of 11,872mm of rain – a boon for the waterfalls that thunder dramatically down the surrounding steep slopes. However, it's nearby Cherrapunjee that declares itself to be the dampest spot of all; to cope, locals traverse the surrounding countryside via 'living bridges' – natural fairytale spans made of rubber-tree roots, which don't wash away in the rain.
Most rain falls during the summer monsoon, which starts by the third week of May and continues to October.

⊙ HEAT HAZE, DEATH VALLEY, USA

El Azizia, Libya, is officially the hottest place on earth, having once pushed the mercury to 57.8°C. But Death Valley runs a close second. The fieriest temperature recorded in this Californian depression (at aptly named Furnace Creek) is 56.7°C; moreover, it's the most consistently sweltering spot anywhere (not to mention

boasting the world's biggest thermometer in nearby Baker, in case you're interested). Despite all this, Death Valley is far from dead: sidewinder rattlesnakes, kangaroo rats, even a species of fish all survive here. And catch it after a rare mini-downpour to see wildflowers put on a brief but brilliant show of colour.

Various ranger-led programs run throughout Death Valley National Park from November to April; see www.nps.gov/deva.

✪ STORMS, VANCOUVER ISLAND, CANADA

Most places keep quiet about their bad weather – it tends to put tourists off. Not so Vancouver Island, which positively revels in the wild wind-lashings and 8m-high wave poundings it receives. From October, a low-pressure system amasses ominously in the Gulf of Alaska, nudging the tempestuous Arctic-meets-subtropical-air front southwards. And this places the British Columbian island right in the path of the resulting storms; from November to February, a gazillion gales smack into the exposed west coast. Spend the winter in Tofino to watch the full Pacific fury. When it's subsided, head out beachcombing, to see what treasures have blown in on the storm's coat-tails.

Tofino, near Pacific Rim National Park, is on the southwest coast of Vancouver Island, a five-hour drive from the capital Victoria.

BEST PLACES
TO GET A TATTOO

WE BRING YOU A LIST OF INK-REDIBLE SPOTS TO GET
A ONE-OF-A-KIND SOUVENIR.

 **WAT BANG PHRA,
THAILAND**

Looking for superhuman powers, such as
the ability to stop a speeding bullet? The
Buddhist monks at Wat Bang Phra can help.
They're known for inking *yantra* tattoos that
bestow the wearer with mystical strength,
protection and good luck. It's not for wimps,
as the holy tattooists carve the monkeys,
tigers and ancient Khmer/Cambodian
designs using a scary 45cm needle. But
hey, if Angelina Jolie can take it, you can
(she's *yantra's* most famous canvas). Each
year in early March the temple holds a wild
tattoo festival where attendees go into
trances and 'become' the animal spirits of
their tattoos.

Wat Bang Phra is in the Nakhon Chai Si
district of Nakhon Pathom province, about
60km west of Bangkok.

 **NORTH ISLAND,
NEW ZEALAND**

Think 'Maori warrior', and an image of
a fierce-looking dude with blue tattoos
swirling across his face appears. In New
Zealand's indigenous culture, the complex
designs – called *ta moko* – represent a
person's identity, origin and bravery. It's
like a history on the skin for those who know
how to read it. Traditionally artists made
their mark using a bone chisel, though
today they tend to use less-painful modern
technology. True *ta moko* is sacred, so if
you're Mike Tyson or otherwise non-Maori,
you can get a similar-type motif called
kirituhi. Auckland and Rotorua are centres
for the art form.

Te Uhi a Mataora is a national collective of
ta moko artists; many are listed at www.
maoriart.org.nz (under Profiles).

**03 HENNA SOUK, FEZ,
MOROCCO**

Henna is the tenderfoot's tattoo: an orange-
red paste that is stencilled on and which
washes away in a few weeks. In Morocco,
women henna their hands and feet with
whirls for weddings, while boys get the job
done before circumcision ceremonies to
protect against evil spirits. Fez has an entire
souk dedicated to the art, tucked into the old

walled medina past the gilt-thread wedding-belt souk and around the corner from the carved-wedding-throne souk. Browse the hennas and lucky-talisman stencils for sale, then settle in with an artist who will paint your hands in the tree-shaded courtyard. The Henna Souk is located off Tala a Kebira and generally opens from 9am to 6pm (closed Friday mornings).

✪ YOKOHAMA TATTOO MUSEUM, YOKOHAMA, JAPAN

Horiyoshi III, arguably the globe's most famous ink man, sets up shop here. He specialises in Japan's age-old, full-body tattoos intertwining dragons, peonies, koi and other mythic images – a process that can take up to five years of weekly visits and cost US$30,000. Tokyo's Yakuza mafia are the most famous practitioners. Tat fans make a pilgrimage to the museum to see underworld photos, traditional tools of the trade and curios that range from shrunken heads to stuffed tigers, and even letters from Charles Manson. Horiyoshi's studio sits above the spooky collection, though he now limits his work to finishing existing clients' tattoos. The museum is located near Yokohama Station in the Imai Building. Hiranuma 1-11-7; it's open from 1pm to 6.30pm daily.

✪ THE BIGGEST TATTOO SHOW ON EARTH, LAS VEGAS, USA

The Guinness World Record–certified name doesn't lie. More than 40,000 tattoo-ees converge at this raucous show in Sin City each year. Big-name international artists wield ink guns on site, so you can offer up skin to a master for whom you'd otherwise

have to travel oceans. Afterward, indulge in an only-in-Vegas establishment located in the same building: King Ink Tattoo Studio & Bar brazenly combines alcohol and body art, all to the thumping beat of a DJ. A little tequila, a little Lady Gaga and the possibilities become endless...
The Biggest Tattoo Show on Earth (www. lasvegastattooshow.com) takes place in October. King Ink (www.kinginklasvegas. com) opens daily at noon.

✪ AMSTERDAM TATTOO MUSEUM, NETHERLANDS
Opened in 2011, the Amsterdam Tattoo Museum holds enough relics to earn its 'Tatican' nickname. The first electric tattoo machine (from 1891), preserved pieces of tattooed flesh, painful-looking tribal implements, freak-show posters and a serious research library stuff the rambling building. Want a memento of your visit? Sure there's the gift shop, but ascend to the second floor where resident artists apply the ultimate keepsake. Note, too, when you patronise the museum you're doing good: the venue provides work experience to 300 socially disadvantaged people per year.
The Amsterdam Tattoo Museum (www. amsterdamtattoomuseum.com) is at Plantage Middenlaan 62; open 10am to 7pm.

✪ MIAMI, USA
The prize for most tatted-up city in the USA goes to Miami, which has about 24 tattoo parlours per 100,000 people. No wonder tattoo reality TV got its start here. *Miami Ink* was the genre's first, following the life and times of five guys working the

scene on South Beach. Assorted porn stars, skateboarders, death metal bands, comedians, film actors and NFL linebackers walked through the door, as did celeb chef Anthony Bourdain (who opted for a skull tattoo on his shoulder). The drama was so intense producers spun off the series to *LA Ink*, *London Ink* and *NYC Ink*.
The *Miami Ink* guys operate LoveHate Tattoo (www.lovehatetattoos.com) at 1360 Washington Avenue; open 11am to 11pm daily.

✪ LONDON TATTOO CONVENTION, ENGLAND
London has had its ink on from the get-go. Pritani, the oldest known name for Britain's inhabitants, means 'the Painted People', after their whopping tattoos. By the end of the 19th century, British sailors were carrying on the custom, with more than 90% drawn upon. So tattoo culture runs deep, and it's why 20,000 people stream in for the convention, keen to take in the tattoo art exhibits, Oxford-curated tattoo historical displays and of course, tattoo contests. Best of Day, Best Back Ornament, Best Colours and Best of Show are just a few prizes to aspire to.
The London Tattoo Convention (www. thelondontattooconvention.com) takes place in late September.

✪ TAHITI, FRENCH POLYNESIA
This is the nation that gave the world tattoos, or at least the word. It comes from the Tahitian *tatau*, 'to strike'. Long ago, artists took a comb with teeth of sharpened bone, dipped the tips into organic black ink, then used a second stick to tap it into

HORIYOSHI THE 3RD, A MASTER TATTOOIST, IN HIS STUDIO IN YOKOHAMA, JAPAN

the skin. The sound it made was *tat tat tat*. Artists mostly use tattoo guns now, but you can opt for the old-school method at many shops. It's more expensive, requiring helpers to stretch your skin while the artist pokes you thousands of times. Turtles (fertility) and tikis (protection) are common symbols. On Sundays in the capital Papeete, local tattoo artists sling ink on the main market's upper level.

✪ DELHI, INDIA

Indian *mehndi* is similar to Moroccan henna – temporary, orange-red tattoos that last a few weeks or so – but artists apply the paisley, peacock and other flowery designs more densely. Women typically henna their hands in an elaborate ceremony before getting married, with the groom's name written somewhere within the pattern. If he can't find it, the bride will have control in the marriage, so the story goes. Beauty parlours have *mehndi* artists on staff, and markets often have *mehndi*-wallahs. The latter are particularly prevalent in Delhi's time-hewn bazaars. *Mehndi*-wallahs cluster around the Shelton Hotel at 5043 Main Bazaar, Paharganj.

SNAKES ALIVE!

OPHIDIOPHILES REJOICE: THE CHINESE YEAR OF THE SNAKE IS UPON US – AN EXCUSE TO EXPLORE THE WORLD'S SCALIEST, SLITHERIEST SPOTS.

01 NARCISSE SNAKE DENS, MANITOBA, CANADA

Twice a year these limestone crevasses and caverns host the world's biggest concentration of serpents – more than 50,000 red-sided garter snakes slithering, swarming and seducing. During the first weeks of May, masses of males emerge from their winter hibernation; frisky in the spring air, they descend in scores on receptive ladies as they appear, forming writhing 'mating balls' – up to 100 males wrestling for the right to mate with each female. For a slightly less intense experience, return in September to see the snakes return to their hibernacula to enter their winter torpor. Narcisse is 130km north of Winnipeg; viewing platforms are spaced along a 3km trail looping around the snake dens. See www.gov.mb.ca/conservation/wildlife/viewing/narcisse.html.

02 EL CASTILLO, CHICHÉN ITZÁ, MEXICO

Make a date with Kukulcán, the feathered serpent-god of the Maya, and head over to his place – the millennium-old step pyramid known as El Castillo at Chichén Itzá, in Mexico's Yucatán. How does 20 March suit? Or perhaps 22 September? On those evenings – the spring and autumn equinoxes – the shadows cast by the setting sun against the northern slope create the illusion of two serpents (whose stone heads guard the base of the staircase) crawling down the pyramid, their slender bodies wriggling down the steps. Visit a day or two either side of the equinox to avoid the biggest crowds.

The site is open 8am to 5pm daily. Day trips from Cancún or Mérida are possible; stay overnight to devote more time to exploring.

03 BASKING ADDERS, DORSET, ENGLAND

Venomous serpents? In Britain? Oh yes: to paraphrase the famous song, mad dogs and English snakes go out in the midday sun – and Dorset's the place to see these beautifully zigzag-patterned vipers basking in sheltered, sun-kissed spots, typically among clumps of heather along

the cliff paths, on commons or in woodland clearings. This southerly county boasts the full complement of the UK's snake species, with rare smooth snakes and larger grass snakes making up the numbers. Walk softly on warm spring days to witness adders, newly woken from hibernation, coiled like ammonites – try Powerstock Common or Fontmell Down for reliable sightings. Dorset Wildlife Trust manages several reserves where adders can be spotted – see www.dorsetwildlifetrust.org.uk.

☉ ANACONDAS, PANTANAL, BRAZIL

There are plenty of big reasons to explore this wet and wild wonderland, which straddles the borders between Brazil, Bolivia and Paraguay: capybara (the world's biggest rodent), jaguars (the Americas' biggest cat), giant river otters (the world's biggest... oh, you guessed?). And then there's the anaconda, the world's heftiest snake – 8m and 200kg-plus of scale-clad muscle. They're not venomous – no, instead they're designed specifically for squeezing the life out of tasty mammals. That'd be you, then... With their beautifully patterned olive-brown skin, full-grown anacondas are entrancing to watch – just don't get too mesmerised, or too close. Watch for basking snakes on the Estrada Parque, a dirt road that runs through the south centre of the Pantanal.

WATCH YOUR STEP: THE ADDER IS ENGLAND'S ONLY (MILDLY) VENOMOUS SNAKE

✪ NAAG PANCHAMI, SOUTH INDIA

Celebrate sacred serpents with fasting and festivities at the height of the monsoon, when flooding forces many snakes from their lairs. Legends connected with the gods – Krishna's defeat of the serpent Kalia, Shiva's reptile companions – inspire offerings of milk and flowers to cobras (both images and real) in the hope of securing protection against snakebites and evil. The festival is celebrated most actively in Maharashtra, West Bengal and the southern states. In 2013 Naag Panchami falls on 11 August.

Head to Mannarsala Temple in Haripad, near Alappuzha, Kerala for year-round snake-worshipping action. See http://mannarasala.org.

✪ TEMPLE DES SERPENTS, OUIDAH, BENIN

Do you do voodoo? If the thought gives you the heebie-jeebies, it might be an idea to give the coastal town of Ouidah a hiss – sorry, a miss. Here, in the heartland of West Africa's traditional religion, the annual Voodoo Festival is celebrated each January with singing, dancing, drinking and sacrifices. Central to the worship of the snake-god Dan (or Dangbé) is the Temple des Serpents, where several dozen royal pythons doze, curled in a hut until needed to communicate with the deity (and ready to be draped over your shoulders by a persuasive guide).

On Benin's Atlantic coast, the Temple des Serpents is typically open from 8am to 7pm.

✪ GREAT SERPENT MOUND, OHIO, USA

Snakes and spirituality are inextricably linked: these death-dealing, egg-laying reptiles allude to both the beginning and end of life, gods and demons, protection and destruction. We don't know why the Great Serpent Mound was built – though alignment with celestial events suggests some astronomical significance – or who built it, or when. Whoever made it, it's impressive: a 420m-long, turf-covered snake coiling through the trees in southern Ohio, mouth gaping to swallow the moon, the sun or perhaps a frog... A marvellous mystery.

The grounds are open daily, sunrise to sunset; the museum opens 10am to 5pm, weekends only in March, November and December (closed January and February).

✪ SNAKE PAGODA, PALEIK, MYANMAR

If a couple of very large snakes decide to take up residence, it pays to be nice to them. That's the philosophy adopted by the monks of the Yadana Labamuni Hsu-taungpye Paya, the pagoda better known as Hmwe Paya, or 'Snake Pagoda'. Here, some 40 years ago, a pair of pythons reportedly appeared, coiled around a statue of Buddha at this temple in Paleik, southwest of Mandalay. Today, their successors are treated with such reverence that the pagoda is virtually a snake spa: the reptiles receive a daily bath in a flower-filled pool, regular feedings and the freedom of the village.

Bath time is 11am daily; do explore the surrounding area, which is littered with hundreds of stupas and pagodas.

✪ RAINBOW SERPENT, KAKADU, AUSTRALIA

In the deepest waterholes lurks a gargantuan snake. Some call her Almudj or Ngalyod, others Myndie or Bunyip; she sings and names places, creates and shapes landscapes, protects and punishes. The Rainbow Serpent is a character that dominates the creation myths of Aboriginal peoples across Australia; where she passed, she left her mark in geological formations and ancient art painted on rocks. At Ubirr, in Kakadu National Park, Northern Territory, astonishing images – some daubed more than 10,000 years ago – recreate legends and daily life. Among them, the Rainbow Serpent, known here as Garranga'rreli, writhes with power in her own rock gallery.

Ubirr is open 8.30am to sunset 1 April to 30 November, 2pm to sunset 1 December to 31 March.

✪ BOA CONSTRICTORS, PALO VERDE NATIONAL PARK, COSTA RICA

A well-fed snake is a happy snake – and everyone prefers to be near a happy snake (hungry, bad-tempered snakes tend not to make the best companions). That's why Isla Pájaros in Costa Rica's Palo Verde National Park is the place to see boa constrictors. The national park attracts the greatest concentration of waterfowl and water birds in Central America – which means nests, eggs and chicks, which means dinner. Spot the serpents from the safety of a boat tour down Río Tempisque, led by a ranger who can point out both reptile predators and avian prey.

Visit in the dry season – in January, water-bird nesting peaks, providing ample food for the boa constrictors.

BEST PLACES TO GET FIT

THEY SAY EVERYONE ALWAYS GAINS WEIGHT ON VACATION. NOT ON THESE ACTIVE ADVENTURES!

01 WILDFITNESS KENYA

Get in touch with your hunter-gatherer roots at this nature-oriented fitness resort, where you'll be instructed in the principles of 'wild moving' (barefoot running, swimming, climbing), 'wild eating' (lots of meats, fruits and vegetables, no dairy or processed foods) and 'wild living' (good sleep habits, 'tribal bonding' with others). The location for all this back-to-BC learning is a palm-shrouded boutique hotel overlooking the white sand and gin-clear waters of the Indian Ocean. So when you're not channelling your inner caveman, you can relax on the roof deck or luxuriate in a deep tissue massage – thanks, modernity! A nine-day course starts at about US$3550. See http://wf.rechord.com.

02 HIKING THE APPALACHIAN TRAIL, USA

Though most 'thru hikers' aren't tackling the 3500km-long Appalachian Trail just to lose a few pounds, it's certainly a side benefit for some. In fact, keeping the weight on while trekking up the sides of heather-shrouded mountains and through rugged green valleys is so difficult that hikers swap tips on the highest-calorie foods to bring along for the journey. Most hikers can pack in 4000 to 6000 calories a day while still losing weight and gaining enough muscle to tackle the killer peaks of Maine's Mt Katahdin at the end of the trail.

The Appalachian Trail begins in Springer Mountain, Georgia and traverses 14 states before ending in Maine. For trail info, see www.appalachiantrail.org.

03 DETOX RETREAT, BAGUS JATI, BALI, INDONESIA

Offering detox regimes promising to cure you of everything from anxiety to bloated stomach to 'vagueness', this New Age-meets-Eastern retreat in Bali's Ubud district will help centre your mind as it slims your waist. Set on a steep emerald hillside, Bagus Jati's Balinese-style villas overlook a lush, misty valley of ferns and betel-nut palms. Daily treatments range from herbal teas to acupuncture to mud

WALK THIS WAY: THE
APPALACHIAN TRAIL, NEW
HAMPSHIRE, USA

wraps. For exercise, get your downward dog on in the round yoga pavilion surrounded by sun-dappled bamboo forest. Or kick it up with a five-hour predawn trek to witness the sunrise from the peak of Mt Batur. Packages start at $620 for two nights; see www.bagusjati.com.

✪ BIKINI BOOTCAMP, TULUM, MEXICO

The setting – a luscious stretch of golden beach on Mexico's Yucatan Peninsula – should take some of the sting out of the butt-kicking daily schedule at this much-imitated fitness retreat. Days begin at 6.45am and hop from gruelling vinyasa yoga classes to sweaty beach volleyball games to power abs workouts. Downtime means swimming in local *cenotes* (water-filled sinkholes) or hiking through the spooky Mayan ruins of Tulum. If you're down with a bit of a New Age-y vibe (think 'tribal drumming' lessons, dawn journaling sessions), then this might be just the place to kick off your New Year's get-fit resolution. Solo travellers are welcome and encouraged.

The Bootcamp is in Tulum, 1½ hours south of Cancun. A six-day session costs US$1950. See www.bikinibootcamp.com.

SURFERS AT BYRON
BAY, AUSTRALIA

✿ SIVANANDA YOGA ASHRAM, THE BAHAMAS

Staying at this jungle retreat on the aptly named Paradise Island means following a few rules, such as committing to eight hours of yoga and meditation a day, and eschewing alcohol, cigarettes and meat. What the ashram lacks in tropical cocktails it makes up for in uber-healthy communal vegetarian meals, massages and Ayurvedic spa treatments, from the postcard-perfect views of the turquoise Atlantic. No need to be a professional yogini to stay here – guests range from Spandex-clad weekend warriors to hardcore devotees.

The ashram is across the bay from downtown Nassau. Accommodation ranges from bare-bones dorms (US$70) to nicely furnished private huts (US$130). See www. sivananda.org.

✿ FATPACKING, VARIOUS LOCATIONS

OK, we're not fond of the name (admittedly, 'CurvyPacking' or 'RubenesquePacking' don't have quite the same ring). But these weight loss-oriented backpacking sessions are a great way to lose a few kilos. Intended for people 7kg to 34kg overweight, the one- to two-week wilderness hikes promise a weight loss of between 2kg and 3kg a week, combined with an increase in muscle mass. Hike locations range from the craggy, cloud-shrouded peaks of Chilean Patagonia to the steamy subtropical swamplands of north Florida to the bewitching red-rock desert of Utah's canyonlands.

Trips start at about US$1000. See www.fatpacking.com.

✪ SURF CAMP AUSTRALIA

Did you ever see a pro surfer with less-than-flat abs? Exactly. Newbies are welcome at this fun-loving Aussie surf school, where you'll learn to ride the waves, and likely tone up your core in the bargain. Days are spent paddling in the sapphire waters of iconic Byron Bay and Seven Mile Beach, while nights mean relaxing at your rustic beach cabin or partying with your instructors. Just take it easy on the free beer, lest you undo a good day's work! Courses run from short-and-sweet three-day weekenders to ten-day Ultimate Surf Adventures.

A three-day camp starts at about A$395 (US$385). See http://surfcamp.com.au.

✪ FOLLOW THE TOUR DE FRANCE

You've watched the Tour de France – why not ride it yourself? Get enviable calf muscles while gawking at the sunflower fields of Provence or the icy knifelike peaks of the Pyrenees. Several companies offer cycling tours of chunks of the competition route – scale the dizzying heights of Mont Ventoux or choose a gentler route through the velvety hills of the Basque Country. Most companies recommend you come with a fairly high level of fitness to begin with – a recreational

cyclist who does a couple of 30km rides a week should be fine. If you get too winded, you can always crash in the sag van.

Trips tend to range from about €2000 to €4000 a week (US$2500–5000).

✪ TRIATHLON TRAINING, PERLA HOTEL, RICCIONE, ITALY

Quick, pick three words to describe an Italian vacation. 'Pizza, pasta, gelato'? How about 'swim, bike, run'? The Perla Hotel, on northern Italy's stately Adriatic Riviera, is one of many in the region that cater to both triathletes and recreational cyclists. Join hotel-led group training rides into the surrounding hills, or just borrow a bike for a casual spin along Riccione's oceanside cycling path. Afterwards, cool off with a quick dip in the navy sea, or take a run down the boardwalk. Hey, with all that training, you can afford a little pizza, pasta and gelato!

Rooms range from budget to luxury. See more at www.perlahotel.com.

✪ THALMAR BIARRITZ, BIARRITZ, FRANCE

If exercise is not your thing, do as the French do: go for a round of thalassotherapy in Biarritz. 'Thalasso-WHAT?', you say? This water treatment involves being wrapped in mud and hosed off with sea water and is très chic among vacationing Parisians. The French consider it medicinal, and many claim it's the secret to their slimness in the face of foie gras and chocolate mousse. We make no promises, but we can say that a stay at the Thalmar will leave you refreshed and glowing.

A three-day getaway starts at about €550 (US$700). See www.biarritz-thalasso.com.

GREAT WALL WALKS

ORIGINALLY BUILT TO DIVIDE, THESE MIGHTY BARRIERS NOW ENABLE EXCELLENT ACCESS ON FOOT.

01 BERLIN WALL, GERMANY

Not so very long ago, this walk was strictly *verboten*. The Berlin Wall – its barbed-wired length manned by armed guards – only fell in 1989. Today, most of the 160km-long barricade that once encircled West Berlin is gone. But it's not forgotten: a marked walk and cycle trail follows its former route, from Potsdamer Platz and Niederkirchnerstrasse (where 200m of wall has been preserved), via Checkpoint Charlie and the Sonnenallee border crossing, out into Berlin's bucolic surrounds. The contrast is stark: pretty lakes and churches – the picture of innocence – are blemished by eerie flecks of crumbling concrete.

The Wall Trail is divided into 14 sections between 7km and 21km long; each section is accessible by public transport.

02 HADRIAN'S WALL, ENGLAND

Roman Emperor Hadrian was a philhellenic soul – a lover of Greek culture. It seems, however, he wasn't so fond of the Scots. From AD 122, he commenced building a barrier of stone, turf, forts and ditches from Wallsend (on the River Tyne) to the shores of the Solway Firth, to demarcate the northernmost reach of his empire. What lay beyond was just too wild to be tamed. And it's *still* pretty wild – Roman remnants sit out amid Cumbrian hills, rough uplands and salt flats. A 140km National Trail navigates the route, and you can imagine the sandal-slap of centurions still audible on the breeze. Hadrian's Wall Trail takes seven days. Segedenum Roman Fort (eastern start/ end point) is a 10-minute Metro ride from Newcastle.

03 GREAT WALL, CHINA

It's hard to walk the whole Great Wall of China. And not just because it's vast (though the fact that it measures around 5000km long presents a significant impediment). No, it's just so disparate, with different bits, from many dynasties, making a conclusive route hard to pinpoint. A classic through-walk is from wild-west Jiayuguan to eastern Shanhaiguan, on the Bohai Sea – a 4000km-plus epic across mountains, steppe and desert. More manageable perhaps is a day-trip from Beijing: the 11km Jinshanling–

Simatai hike has fine far-reaching views; the little-known 12km stretch at Huanghuacheng is really wild wall walking.

Visit from September to October or April to May for the best weather and avoid busy Chinese national holidays (first weeks of May and October).

⊙ CARTAGENA, COLOMBIA

Strolling atop the 16th-century fortifications that cloister old Cartagena is the best way to get a feel for this Unesco-listed city. It's a place that deserves protection – initially for its strategic importance to the Spanish, now for its comely cobbles and pastel prettiness. It's not a long walk along the thick *murallas* (the whole loop takes about 90 minutes) but it is a beauty. Start from Balaurte de San Francisco Javier at sunset, to watch the warm light glitter on the Caribbean and set Cartagena's yellow-pink mansions, palm-fringed plazas and profusion of churches aglow.

The wall stands in four sections; the Balaurte de San Francisco Javier–La India Catalina section is longest.

✪ ÁVILA, SPAIN

Approach by train from nearby Madrid and it seems that a colossal sandcastle has been made on the high plains of Castilla y Léon. The almost-too-perfectly walled city of Ávila looms large and castellated, its old centre enclosed within 2.5km of 12m-high, 3m-thick stone; 88 towers and nine gates ensure it looks properly fairytale. These are the best-preserved medieval walls in the world, and much of them can be strolled along. That said, arguably the best views are *extra-muros* – leave the city confines to walk around the outside, to see the defences in all their intimidating, impenetrable glory.

Ávila is 1130m above sea-level; it can get cold, even in summer, so pack warm clothes.

✪ OFFA'S DYKE, ENGLAND–WALES

You've heard of Hadrian, but who on earth was Offa? King of Mercia, that's who; he ruled most of England in AD 757, but Wales was another matter. Unable to best those feisty dragons, he built a wall to keep them out. Well, not a wall – more a ditch, backed by a mound of mud (more interesting than it sounds...). Offa's Dyke National Trail traces these ancient remains, wending 285km from Sedbury Cliffs to Prestatyn, via the Black Mountains, book-town Hay-on-Wye and the heather-clad Clwydian Range, traversing a land that still feels like a wild frontier.

Offa's Dyke National Trail takes around 12 days to complete. Chepstow train station is 1.6km from Sedbury Cliffs.

✪ ESSAOUIRA, MOROCCO

The ramparts ringing Atlantic-slapped Essaouira aren't the world's longest or biggest. But they do have a certain superstar status. In 1949 Orson Welles came to town and filmed the Moroccan city's walls for the opening sequence of his movie, *Othello*. There's certainly drama here: built in the 18th century by Sultan Mohammed III, who was keen to own a coastal stronghold, these Vauban-style defences perch on sea cliffs. Walk along their parapet to look down on the rambling medina within – a huddle of slipper-sellers, tagine-makers and labyrinthine alleys – and to look out over the harbour and golden beach beyond.

Essaouira is a 2½-hour bus ride from Marrakesh and a six-hour journey from Casablanca.

✪ QUÉBEC CITY, CANADA

Architecture often isn't that old in North America. Which makes the 17th-century walls surrounding Québec City all the more notable. The capital of Canada's Gallic province is a bit 'France-lite': there's European flair in the higgledy streets, *frites* served in the cafes and history sunk deep into these great grey military fortifications. The whole wall is 4.6km long, incised by gates and bulged by towers. At times you can stand atop it, to look across to the St Lawrence River and down on the huddled alleys of Vieux Québec; at others, stroll alongside to feel just how impervious a barrier it still is.

Parks Canada runs guided, 90-minute wall tours, departing from the Frontenac kiosk on Dufferin Terrace.

✪ WALLS OF JERUSALEM NATIONAL PARK, AUSTRALIA

Australia is far from the Holy Land, but explorers with a Biblical bent let rip when they assigned names to this corner of Tasmanian countryside – Herod's Gate stands by the Walls of Jerusalem, the Pool of Bethesda and Solomon's Jewels. The 'walls' are dolerite hills, topping at the 1509m King David's Peak, in a people-free landscape of conifer forest and heath. There are no roads so bushwalking is the only way to worship here. Follow the track from Lake Rowallan to Dixons Kingdom and up Mt Jerusalem for views over this antipodean Eden.

Walls of Jerusalem is not accessible by road; visitors must walk in from the car park off Mersey Forest Rd, near Lake Rowallan.

✪ AURELIAN WALLS, ROME, ITALY

In AD 270, Emperor Aurelius got a bit twitchy. With barbarians threatening from the north, he decided to encircle Rome with a big brick barricade. And he did it fast: this 19km-long, 6.5m-high obstacle – boasting 381 towers and 18 gates – was constructed in just five years. Today it's tatty in places; in 2001 a 12m section collapsed; 2007 saw another stretch fall. But considering its venerable age, it remains impressive. One of the best-preserved bits is by Porta San Sebastiano, where the parapet is strollable, and offers fine views; the keen history-hiker could get a map and trace the entire route. The Museo delle Mura, on Via di Porta San Sebastiano, is inside the walls' Sebastiano Gate; entrance costs €4 (US$5).

LEGENDARY LAST STANDS

STAND IN THE SPOTS WHERE SOME OF THE WORLD'S MOST FAMOUS AND INFAMOUS FIGURES CAME TO UNTIMELY ENDS.

01 SAN VICENTE, BOLIVIA

A last stand? Or a red herring? There's some doubt surrounding the deaths of Robert LeRoy Parker and Harry Longabaugh – aka Butch Cassidy and the Sundance Kid. These American bandits were supposedly gunned down in dusty San Vicente: a stand-off in the village in 1908 certainly resulted in two gringo corpses riddled with bullets. They were buried in the local cemetery, but no formal identification was ever made – some claim the duo were alive and well years later. You can still follow the Butch and Sundance trail around southern Bolivia however, including the adobe hut where it all ended. Perhaps...

San Vicente is 100km northwest of Tupiza; local tour agencies run two-day jeep trips to the sites.

02 THERMOPYLAE, GREECE

For King Leonidas of Sparta, Thermopylae ('the Hot Gates') was an all-too-real gateway to hell. It was here, in 480 BC, that he lingered defiantly with a handful of warriors (some say just 300) to defend Greece from 30,000-odd invading Persians. He was slain, eventually, but succeeded in delaying the intruders in a battle that's now a byword for bravery in the face of outrageous odds. The sea has retreated 4km since that time, making Thermopylae a less strategically important defile. But Leonidas stands here still: his heroic statue watches over the burial mound of his courageous comrades.

Thermopylae is on the motorway, just south of Lamía; trains from Athens to Lianokládhi (6km from Lamía) take 2½ hours.

03 TENOCHTITLÁN, MEXICO CITY, MEXICO

In what was less a last stand than a last stand-by-and-watch, Moctezuma II did little to stop Cortés and his conquistadores from raiding the Aztec capital of Tenochtitlán in 1519. Indeed, he invited Cortés in, thinking the Spaniard a fair-skinned god. The result? Moctezuma was killed by his own people, who couldn't bear his passivity. Cortés razed Tenochtitlán; now, Mexico City sprawls over the top. However, in 1978 ruins of the ancient site's Templo Mayor were discovered, right in the heart of the modern metropolis; its stone pyramid, altar of toads and wall of skulls are all reminders of glories past.

The entrance to the Templo Mayor site and museum is beside the cathedral; the site is closed on Mondays.

✪ LITTLE BIG HORN, MONTANA, USA

The Battle of Little Big Horn, or the Battle of Greasy Grass if you're of Native American descent, is famed for being Custer's Last Stand. Though the Unionist general did lose his life combating Chief Sitting Bull on the Montana plains in June 1876, this legendary ruckus really did more damage to the Sioux and Cheyenne he was fighting: victorious on the day, the Indians lost the struggle for their nomadic traditions soon after. Today you can walk round the historic site and to the very spot where Custer finally fell.

Little Big Horn National Monument is 100km south of Billings. Native American guided tours are available May to September; see www.nps.gov/libi.

A DANCER DRESSED AS AN AZTEC WARRIOR AT TEMPLO MAYOR, MEXICO CITY

RORKE'S DRIFT & ISANDLWANA, SOUTH AFRICA

Rorke's Drift – that's the one where Michael Caine faced down 4000 marauding Zulus, no? Not quite. The epic 1964 movie *Zulu*, depicting the plucky resistance of a British garrison against a horde of spear-waving locals, is not entirely historically accurate. It's true to say that the 140 men who, in January 1879, defended their remote post in rugged KwaZulu-Natal were massively outnumbered yet ultimately triumphant. But it's also true that the Battle of Isandlwana, just hours earlier, had a very different outcome, with the Zulus besting the Brits. Museums now stand at both sites, while Isandlwana Hill is peppered with memorials, marking where each soldier fell.

Isandlwana (70km southeast of Dundee) and Rorke's Drift are 15km apart; a dirt road connects the two.

CAJAMARCA, PERU

It shouldn't have been this way. Atahualpa had 500 times more men than conquistador Pizarro. But, in 1532, the well-armed Spaniard managed to massacre thousands of indigenous people in Cajamarca – and capture the Inca Emperor in the process. Atahualpa was imprisoned in the *Cuarto del Rescate* (Ransom Chamber), the only Inca building still standing in this northern highlands city. And though he collected enough gold and silver to buy his freedom, he was executed anyway, hung in the main square – on the site of Cajamarca's modern-day Plaza de Armas – in what marked the beginning of the end of the Inca Empire.

Cuarto del Rescate is open 9am to 1pm and 3pm to 6pm daily; entrance includes the Belén church and hospital complex and Ethnographic Museum.

BATTLE, ENGLAND

Other last stands may have been immortalised in movies, but Harold II's final throes were given a much classier commemoration. The 70m-long Bayeux Tapestry gives an embroidered rundown of events leading up to 1066 and the Battle of Hastings, where King Harold of England was slain by a Norman arrow. The tapestry may be in France, but all the action occurred in Sussex, at Senlac Hill – now site of the appropriately named town of Battle. To mark his famous victory, William the Conqueror built the Abbey of St Martin here, its altar reputedly placed on the very spot where Harold floundered.

Battle of Hastings Abbey and the battlefield is managed by English Heritage. Entrance costs £7.30 (US$11.50); see www.english-heritage.org.uk.

GIBSLAND, LOUISIANA, USA

There's a small grey marker by the side of Highway 154, 8km south of Gibsland, Louisiana. It reads 'On This Site, May 23, 1934, Clyde Barrow and Bonnie Parker Were Killed By Law Enforcement Officers'. It may read other things, too – it is often daubed with graffiti (from couples on, it seems, odd romantic pilgrimages); also, bullet-holes pock its surface. Such defacing seems fitting: Bonnie and Clyde had little

respect for property themselves. But the pair are still weirdly lauded, and Gibsland's Ma Canfield's Cafe – where they dined their last – is now a museum devoted to America's first 'celebrity' criminals.
The Bonnie & Clyde Ambush Museum, in Gibsland, is open daily (except Wednesdays), admission is $7/5 adult/child; see www. bonnieandclydemuseum.com.

✪ ISTANBUL, TURKEY

It had lasted for more than a thousand years, so Emperor Constantine XI wasn't going to give up on the Byzantine Empire

easily – even if its time was clearly up. When Ottoman Sultan Mehmed II came to conquer Constantinople (today's Istanbul) in 1453, the emperor fought to the death alongside his soldiers on the city's land walls. There are still remnants of those defences – largely crumbly – to the west of the old town. Also here, Yedikule Fort is more solid; according to Greek legend, Constantine is buried under its Golden Gate, waiting to be resurrected to reclaim the city for Christendom.
Yedikule Fort can be reached by train from Sirkeci station or by bus from Taksim and Beyazit.

BEST PLACES TO HUNT FOR BURIED TREASURE

THERE'S A SECRET WORLD OF GOODIES BURIED BENEATH THE EARTH'S ROCKS AND WAVES. LOOKING FOR LOOT – FROM PIRATE BOOTY TO SECRET STASHES – IS AN ADVENTURE ALL ITS OWN.

01 OPAL MINING, COOBER PEDY, AUSTRALIA

Outback adventure and the chance to strike it rich: can you dig it? The good folk of Coober Pedy can... and have done, ever since opal was first discovered there in 1915. Named from the local aboriginal term 'kupa-piti' (meaning 'whitefella in a hole'), this far-flung town is known as the opal capital of the world; it's also famous for its underground homes, excavated to escape the desert sizzle. While hardcore miners need a government permit, anyone is allowed to fossick – in local parlance, 'noodle' – through the town's many mine dumps. Don't let the whimsical verb fool you: many a noodler has hit paydirt. Before going it alone, try a sanctioned noodle at Tom's Working Opal Mine (www.tomsworkingopalmine.com.au) or Old Timers' Mine (www.oldtimersmine.com).

02 NORMAN ISLAND, BRITISH VIRGIN ISLANDS

Peg-legs, black spots, West Country accents: if there was a map showing the home of every pirate cliché known to fancy-dressers, Norman Island would be marked with an X. Not shivering your timbers? Perhaps its fictional name, Treasure Island, will make you go 'aaargh'. The inspiration behind Robert Louis Stevenson's tale of mutiny and booty, Norman Island today is a haven for snorkellers and nature lovers. But rumours of undiscovered doubloons hidden in the Caves – a series of aptly murky watery caverns – attract rum-hoisters convinced the island remains home to 'plenty of prizes and plenty of duff!'. Norman Island is a short boat trip from Tortola, the biggest and most populated of the BVIs. Tortola is reached via ferries or flights out of various Caribbean hubs. See www.normanisland.com.

---

03 OAK ISLAND, NOVA SCOTIA, CANADA

Home to a huge, mysterious hole nicknamed the Money Pit, this otherwise unremarkable island is *the* destination for those answering the call of booty. First discovered in 1795, the cryptic Pit is the site of the world's longest-running treasure hunt... although just which treasure is being hunted remains the cause of frenzied debate. Rumoured riches hidden within the hole (which supposedly runs at least 60m deep) include Captain Kidd's stash, the lost jewels of Marie Antoinette, documents proving the 'real' identity of Shakespeare (Francis Bacon, FYI) and the holy grail of treasure seekers, the, erm, Holy Grail. Beware the booby traps!

Oak Island is privately owned and permission is required before setting off to solve the mystery of the Pit. Start here for legends and links; www.oakislandtreasure.co.uk.

✪ GEOCACHING, LAS VEGAS, USA

Cache-ING! Looking for loot in Las Vegas? Forget fruit machines and bank breaking: these days, thousands of Sin City visitors are forgoing gambling for geocaching. A real-life treasure hunt that relies on GPS and cryptic clues, geocaching is more likely to yield a Kinder Egg than that of the nest variety, but that hasn't stopped five million enthusiasts worldwide. Vegas has become a must-do for the high-tech hobbyists, with more than 2400 stashes hidden in and around the city, including scores on the Strip, in the surrounding desert and in spooky spots for 'haunted' night caching. Head to www.nevadageocaching.com and www.geocaching.com for the lowdown on what lies beneath.

✪ GOLD DETECTING, PAPUA NEW GUINEA

There's gold in them thar hills... and on them thar islands... and under that thar sea. Papua New Guinea is absolutely awash with the shiny stuff, and while much of it falls into the hands of multinational mining companies, there's no reason the budding prospector can't have a pick or a pan as well. Gold fever peaked in the 20th century, with nuggets the 'size of goose eggs' attracting feverish prospectors, including a certain Mr Errol Flynn. These days, PNG's rough-and-tumble landscape (social and geographic) make

ROMAN HOARD;
UNEARTH ANCIENT
COINS IN ENGLAND

joining an organised tour a better idea than striking out on your own. They're not cheap, but with a potential 'Eureka!' moment lurking beneath every step, who cares?

PNG Gold Tours offers fully escorted, two-week gold-hunting trips to Misma Island, an area renowned for rich alluvial deposits. Visit www.pnggoldtours.com.

☉ ROMAN COINS, ENGLISH COUNTRYSIDE

Either togas suffered from a lack of pockets or departing Romans hadn't time to stop at a currency exchange, because England is aglitter with ancient currency. And it's yours for the picking. Amateur archaeologists and quaint folk with metal detectors have been responsible for massive finds across the island; in 2010, a chef uncovered a pot filled with 52,000 coins dated between AD 253 and 293, the largest such hoard

yet discovered. Study up, be sure to get landowners' permission and you too could hold history in your hands!

Contact the National Council for Metal Detecting for information on detector hire, regional clubs and valuing your treasure: www.ncmd.co.uk.

☉ DIGGING FOR DINOS, AUSTRALIA

Thrilled by theropods? Is 'muttaburrasaurus' more than just an amusing tongue-twister to you? Then it's a fair bet that joining a dinosaur dig is your idea of the ultimate treasure hunt. And where better to pander to your inner palaeontologist than outback Winton, home to Australia's largest hoard of dino bones? The not-for-profit organisation Australian Age of Dinosaurs holds tri-annual Dinosaur Discovery Weeks, giving enthusasauruses the chance to excavate, plaster and prep fossils buried for the past 95 million years. No experience is necessary, but only 13 spots per dig are available. Book quickly: they'll be gone before you can say 'Diamantinasaurus matildae'.

Digs run between July and September. Find out more and reserve your spot at www. australianageofdinosaurs.com/aa-dig-a-dino.php.

✪ ARCTIC AMETHYSTS, KOLA PENINSULA, RUSSIA

Far above the Arctic Circle, all that glitters is not ice: western Russia's extreme north sparkles with the purple slivers of the prized amethyst. The rugged Kola Peninsula – a mineralogist's dream with its hundreds of rare rock and metal species – is home to the windswept, amethyst-rich Tersky Coast. Unlike gold, the amethyst is surprisingly easy to find if you know where to look (Tersky's Korabl Cape – 'Ship Cape' – is a great place to start): simply look for the purple clumps. In addition to its beauty, amethyst has a legendary quality which may come in handy in these frozen, vodka-loving lands: it's believed to protect its bearer from drunkenness.

While spotting amethysts is simple enough, getting around Kola Peninsula is not. Consider joining a mineralogical tour with the South Kola group (www.kolaklub.com/southkola/mne.htm) or Kola Travel (http://kolatravel.com/mineralogical_holidays.htm).

✪ FOSSIL GAWKING, GOBI DESERT, MONGOLIA

To the hurried eye, the vast Gobi Desert looks like 1.3 million sq km of dusty nothing. But stop, stoop and focus: the Gobi is one of the world's richest fossil depositories, with many ancient (as in 100-million-years-ancient) remains lying only centimetres from the surface. It was here the first dinosaur eggs were discovered; other major excavated finds include rare, mid-evolutionary birds and some of the world's best-preserved mammal fossils. Hunting hotspots include the Flaming Hills of Bayanzag and Altan Uul ('Golden Mountain'). You're not supposed to take your finds home with you – they're rightfully considered national treasures – but here, especially, the thrill is in the chase. Independent (not package) tours can be hard to stumble across, but not impossible. Many guesthouses in Mongolia's capital Ulaanbaatar can help get your expedition underway.

✪ WRECK DIVING, FLORIDA, USA

It may be known as the Sunshine State, but many of Florida's richest attractions haven't seen the light of day in centuries. Thought to be home to more sunken treasure than any other state in the USA, Florida's blue waters may be hiding more than US$200 million worth of loot. Now home to Disneyworld and pampered retirees, the state was once a notorious pirate haven (even Blackbeard dropped anchor here), and its hurricanes sent countless Spanish galleons to Davy Jones' locker. Check local legalities before you wriggle into your wettie, and never dive alone in Florida's oft-treacherous waters: those wrecks are down there for a reason. The website www.treasuresites.com/indexn.htm is a treasure trove of super-detailed listings of potentially enriching (and legal) wreck-dive spots across Florida.

ODDEST FOOD MUSEUMS

FROM CURRY SAUSAGES TO FERMENTED CABBAGE, THIS SELECTION OF SHRINES TO HUMBLE AND STRANGE FOODSTUFFS WILL TITILLATE YOUR TASTEBUDS.

01 CURRYWURST MUSEUM, BERLIN, GERMANY

Sausages have long been a popular German food, but what's the connection with curry? Enterprising Berliner Herta Heuwer obtained curry powder from British troops after WWII, then mixed it with ketchup to create a sauce that was a hit on top of *wurst*. Now this iconic Berlin snack has been given its very own museum. You can simulate the experience of running a currywurst stall, learn about the history of Heuwer's original sauce, and view clips of German film and TV characters scoffing currywurst onscreen. Enter the Spice Chamber... if you dare.

The best-value option is the Snack Ticket costing adult €13.90 (US$17.50), including entry and a serve of currywurst. Visit www. currywurstmuseum.de.

02 PICK SALAMI & PAPRIKA MUSEUM, SZEGED, HUNGARY

You should never enquire too closely into how a sausage is made, and the same is probably true for salami. However, who could resist buying a ticket to a salami museum in a country famous for this tasty food? Within the Pick Salami & Paprika Museum, captions explain how salami is made, next to displays of industrial equipment operated by dummies wearing overalls, enormous moustaches and cloth caps. The upstairs section is devoted to paprika, the ever-present spice in Hungarian food. Price of entry includes a sample of the in-house salami.

The museum is only open from 3pm to 6pm from Tuesday to Saturday, so pick your arrival time carefully. More details at www. pickmuzeum.hu.

03 SHINYOKOHAMA RAUMEN MUSEUM, YOKOHAMA, JAPAN

The popular noodle dish ramen (sometimes spelled raumen) can be found across Japan in a dazzling array of regional variations. It's often topped with pork, fish, dried seaweed or green onions. This museum, which styles itself as a 'food amusement park', features a replica of a Tokyo streetscape of 1958, the year in which instant noodles were invented. However, this is the best type of food museum – the type in which you can eat the food. Within its walls are branches of ramen restaurants from across Japan, serving their own unique take on the tasty dish. *Itadakimasu!*

A one-off adult ticket is ¥300 (US$4), but if you're really keen a three-month pass is ¥500 (US$6). See www.raumen.co.jp.

✪ SPAM MUSEUM, AUSTIN, USA

In the days before unsolicited email, the Monty Python comedy team had fun creating a song in homage to this mundane processed pork product. Derived from the words 'spiced ham', canned Spam was first manufactured in 1937 and is celebrated in this museum in its home town of Austin, Minnesota. Within, you can learn about Spam's heroic role in WWII, peruse old-fashioned advertising, have a go at canning the foodstuff and watch a movie about it. And it's all for free. Just don't spam your friends about it when you get home.

Swing by the Spam Museum from 10am to 5pm Monday to Saturday and from noon to 5pm on Sunday. Find out more at www.spam.com/spam-101/the-spam-museum.

✪ PULMUONE KIMCHI MUSEUM, SEOUL, SOUTH KOREA

Kimchi, usually made from spiced-up, fermented cabbage, is an omnipresent dish in Korea. The crunch of the cabbage is complemented by the heat from red chillies,

DEUTSCHES CURRYWURST MUSEUM (GERMAN CURRY SAUSAGES MUSEUM), BERLIN, GERMANY

and the result is a side dish that goes well with all Korean cuisine. The Pulmuone Kimchi Museum celebrates this everyday food and its cultural pre-eminence via displays on its history, its many varieties, its regional variations and the jars it's been stored in during the centuries. If you're really keen, you can watch a film on how to make more than 80 types of kimchi.

The museum is located beneath the COEX Mall, 159 Samseong-dong, Gangnam-gu. Visitor guide at www.kimchimuseum.co.kr.

✪ JELL-O GALLERY, LEROY, USA

When carpenter Pearle Wait invented a simple gelatine-based dessert in his home in LeRoy, New York in 1897, he had no idea how big his wobbly invention would get. He sold his recipe, and in the hands of clever

marketers, Jell-O became a hit in the early 20th century. Recipe books were widely distributed, as the USA and eventually the world enthused over the just-add-water treat. The Jell-O Gallery presents displays on the history of the foodstuff, focusing on the stars of TV and radio who've promoted it over the years. There's also a gift shop packed with jelly-related memorabilia. The gallery is located between Rochester and Buffalo. For a map and opening hours, see www.jellogallery.org.

✪ FRIETMUSEUM, BRUGES, BELGIUM

'Do you want fries with that?' might be one of life's most mundane questions, but you can't help but say yes when visiting this institution. Those humble fried strips of potato may be known as 'French fries' in the USA, but this museum insists that they originated in Belgium. Within are displays on the history of the potato, fries and the sauces that Belgians like to put on them. The 14th-century building itself is part of the attraction, being a classic example of Bruges' historic charms. You can even sample fries and other Belgian dishes here. The museum is only 300m from the Central Market Place and its famous belfry. Adult admission is €6 (US$7.50); see www.frietmuseum.be.

✪ SU NO SATO VINEGAR MUSEUM, HANDA, JAPAN

Vinegar has long been sprinkled on fish and chips in Britain, but it's also been a popular condiment in Japan since the 5th century. In Handa, south of Nagoya, vinegar was created as a by-product of sake brewing, and the small town became prosperous by exporting it to Tokyo. Today Handa is home to the Su No Sato Vinegar Museum, adjacent to the Mizkan vinegar factory. Exhibits explain the history of vinegar making and its healthy aspects, along with traditional utensils used in its creation. A fermentation room demonstrates how to make the best vinegar.

From Nagoya, catch a train to Obu, then switch to Handa. The museum is at 2-6 Nakamura-cho, open daily from 9am to 4pm.

✪ BURLINGAME MUSEUM OF PEZ MEMORABILIA, SAN FRANCISCO, USA

Pez consists of small brick-shaped pieces of confectionery, invented in 1927 by Austrian businessman Eduard Haas – but the taste isn't what makes this sweet treat stand out. Its claim to fame derives from its novelty dispensers, often shaped like celebrities or fictional characters. The rarer examples are hugely collectable, selling for thousands of dollars, and this museum holds one of the widest collections. Check out dispenser heads ranging from Wonder Woman to Miss Piggy, along with a specially made 2.4m-high dispenser.

Located between San Francisco International Airport and the San Mateo Bridge, next to Burlingame Avenue train station. Details at www.burlingamepezmuseum.com.

✪ EUROPEAN ASPARAGUS MUSEUM, SCHROBENHAUSEN, GERMANY

Germans go crazy for asparagus. Visit the country in springtime and you'll find restaurants breathlessly promoting their chefs' dishes involving the fibrous vegetable. The green version is good, but Germans wax even more lyrical about the thicker white asparagus. The Spargelzeit (asparagus season) each year provokes much celebration, including public events. This museum, located within a medieval tower in Bavaria, houses a wide-ranging set of exhibits on asparagus, covering such aspects as its farming, history, health benefits and cultural significance. It even has a painting of asparagus by Andy Warhol.

The museum can be found at Am Hofgraben 3, Schrobenhausen. Adult admission is €5 (US$6), which includes other city-run museums.

INDEX

ACKNOWLEDGEMENTS

PUBLISHING DIRECTOR Piers Pickard
PUBLISHER Ben Handicott
COMMISSIONING EDITOR &
PROJECT MANAGER Robin Barton
ART DIRECTION & DESIGN Mark Adams
LAYOUT DESIGNER Paul Iacono
EDITORS Kate Whitfield, Kate James
IMAGE RESEARCHERS Rebecca Skinner,
Nicholas Colicchia, Aude Vauconsant
PRE-PRESS PRODUCTION Ryan Evans
PRINT PRODUCTION Larissa Frost

WRITTEN BY Brett Atkinson, Sarah Baxter,
Ryan Ver Berkmoes, Joe Bindloss, Abigail Blasi,
Jean-Bernard Carillet, Laura Crawford,
Leslie Davisson, Tom Hall, Amy Karafin,
Shawn Low, Emily Matchar, Craig McLachlan,
Carolina Miranda, Kate Morgan, Brandon Presser,
Tim Richards, Brendan Sainsbury, Dan Savary Raz,
Andrea Schulte-Peevers, Tamara Sheward,
Oliver Smith, Caroline Veldhuis,
Ryan Ver Berkmoes, Luke Waterson, Tony Wheeler,
Rob Whyte, Rafael Wlodarski, Karla Zimmerman

FOREWORDS BY Hilary Bradt, Tremayne Carew
Pole, Bill Dalton, Mark Ellingham, Stefan Loose,
Tony Wheeler

THANKS TO Patrick Kinsella, Imogen Hall,
Heather Howard, Wibowo Rusli, Marg Toohey

Best in Travel starts with hundreds of ideas from
everyone at Lonely Planet, including our extended family
of travellers, bloggers and tweeters. Once we're confident
we have the cream of 2013's travel choices, the final
selection is made by a panel of in-house travel experts,
based on topicality, excitement, value and that special
X-factor. Our focus is on the merits of each destination
and the unique experiences they offer travellers.

Front Cover Image Corsica - Douglas Pearson/Getty Images

October 2012
ISBN 978 1 74220 999 9
Published by Lonely Planet Publications Pty Ltd
ABN 36 005 607 983
90 Maribyrnong St, Footscray,
Victoria, 3011, Australia
www.lonelyplanet.com

Printed in Singapore
10 9 8 7 6 5 4 3 2 1
© Lonely wPlanet 2012
© Photographers as indicated 2012

LONELY PLANET OFFICES

AUSTRALIA Locked Bag 1, Footscray, Victoria, 3011
Phone 03 8379 8000
Email talk2us@lonelyplanet.com.au

USA 150 Linden St, Oakland, CA 94607
Phone 510 250 6400 Toll free 800 275 8555
Email info@lonelyplanet.com

UK Media Centre, 201 Wood Lane, London W12 7TQ
Phone 020 8433 1333
Email go@lonelyplanet.co.uk

Although the authors and Lonely Planet have taken all
reasonable care in preparing this book, we make no warranty
about the accuracy or completeness of its content and, to the
maximum extent permitted, disclaim all liability from its use.

MIX
Paper from
responsible sources
FSC™ C021741

Paper in this book is certified against
the Forest Stewardship Council™
standards. FSC™ promotes
environmentally responsible, socially
beneficial and economically viable
management of the world's forests.

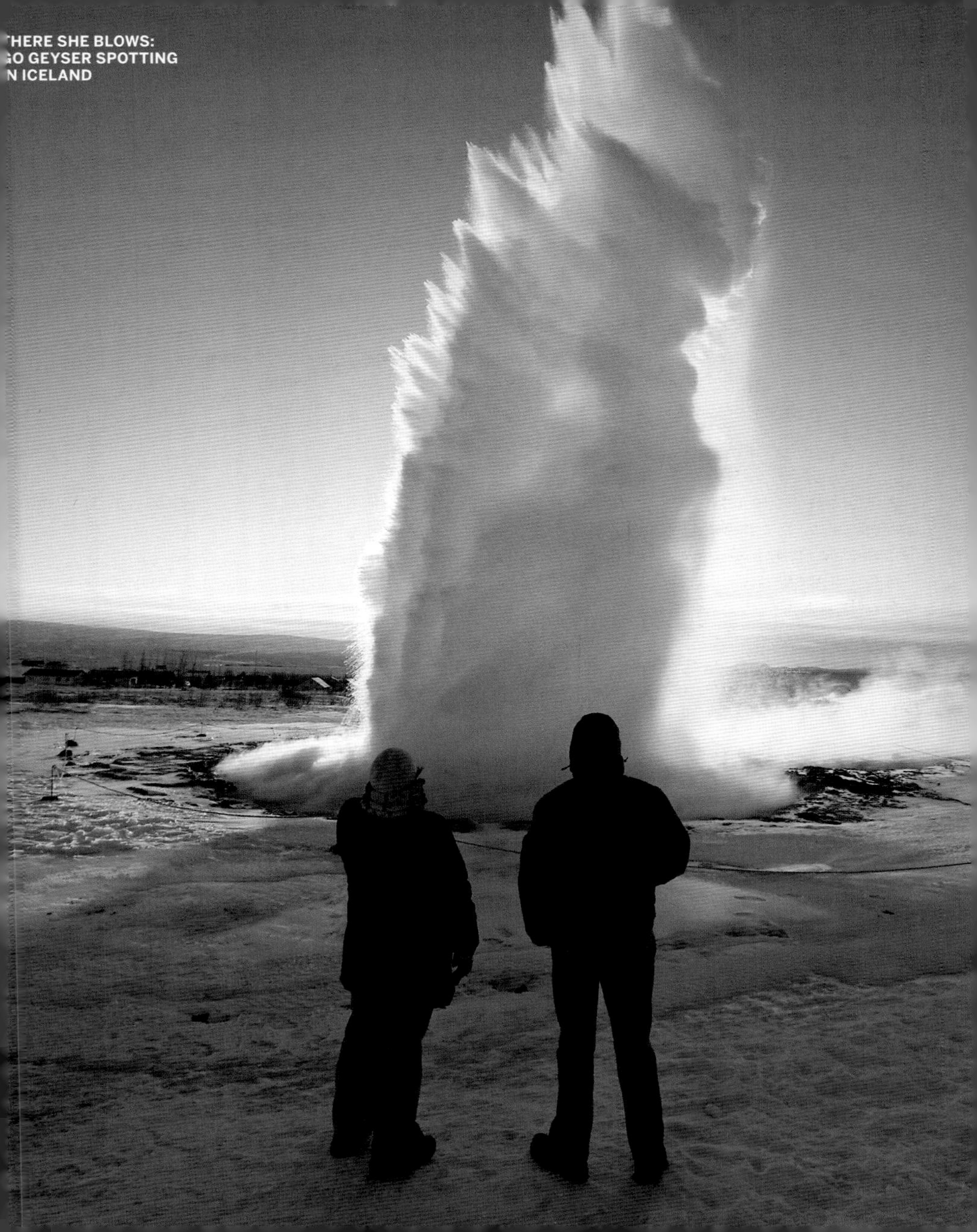

THERE SHE BLOWS: GO GEYSER SPOTTING IN ICELAND

LONELY PLANET'S BEST IN TRAVEL

TRAVEL PLANNER 2013

JANUARY

MONA FOMA, AUSTRALIA Ex-Violent Femmes bassist, Brian Ritchie, curates MONA FOMA, a music and arts festival in Hobart. Past performers include PJ Harvey, The Saints, John Cale and Grandmaster Flash.

SPECIAL OLYMPICS WINTER GAMES, SOUTH KOREA In January and February, Pyeongchang hosts the Special Olympics Winter Games. There will be 3300 athletes competing in 32 events including skiing and snowboarding. It's South Korea's largest ever winter sporting event.

GALLE LITERARY FESTIVAL, SRI LANKA Celebrate the enduring impact of the printed word at January's annual Galle Literary Festival. Past bookish visitors to the heritage fort town's storied streets include Orhan Pamuk, Pico Iyer and Alexander McCall Smith.

FEBRUARY

CARNIVAL, DOMINICAN REPUBLIC Carnival is celebrated all month long. The final blow-out fiesta is held the last weekend in February. It's a raucous dance party, street festival and heated costume competition all rolled into one.

MARDI GRAS, USA The Gulf is renowned for its Mardi Gras celebrations and nowhere else are they as rambunctious, licentious or openly drunken as in New Orleans. This year, the big party falls on February 12.

YUKON QUEST, CANADA The legendary Yukon Quest 1600km dog-sled race goes from Whitehorse to Fairbanks, Alaska through February darkness and -50°C temps.